cannabis*café*

recipes for recreational and therapeutic use

BY ERIC

cannabis*café*

Written by Sam Peacefull-Day, better known to most of us as ERIC.

None of which would have been possible without the wonderful help of family and friends all of whom are very much part of this book.

Thanks to Dave and his bank account
"Roll another fat one babe as I think you are going to need it".

And a special thanks to our photographers
Mike Buchan (cover, food and plant images)
and Mike Mayhem (big buds).

Andrew Garret the curator of the internet's Medicinal Cannabis Picture Museum (bottles) and everyone who shared their words with us or welcomed us into their kitchens.

Published in the United Kingdom by Eric's Kitchen
1st Printing Year 2003
The First Edition
Editing by Debs and Sophie
Proofreading by Piwi and Ian

Printed in Somerset, England

Design by Rhiannon Sully

Distribution Counter Culture

ISBN 0-9529299-2-9

ERIC'S KITCHEN

www.erics-kitchen.co.uk

NOTICE TO READERS

This book is for educational use only. It is not a self-treatment manual.
This book does not attempt to offer an alternative to orthodox
medicine, or to encourage the illegal use of cannabis.

Not for use by or sale to minors

A hairy skunk

Contents

Indian sativa

This book is dedicated to all those around the world who have stood up for the basic right to grow and consume the cannabis plant.

The table set

A taste of the forbidden

The secret ingredient

A feast before your very eyes

Let's join the fantasy and ride

Feast or fantasy?

Introduction

It's a pleasure both to introduce this special collection of Eric's delicious recipes and to be offered the chance to re-acquaint myself with a few old favourites.

Eric and I met one year, (don't ask me which), at a particularly muddy Glastonbury festival. She emerged through the drizzle and tempted me with some truffles. Somehow those innocent looking treats had the power to make the storm clouds part and allow the sunshine in. Levitating above the mire, I soon became infused with the true festival spirit. Although my shoe was lost in the mud, I did make a valuable new friend.

In the pages that follow you will find me making those truffles. Believe me it is a rare treat: as the last time I cooked was in 19...??, and it took me two days! Now you can hardly get me out of the kitchen, and my culinary phenomenon is captured for all to see.

Please excuse me now: Eric's passion for good tasting food laced with quality cannabis is just beginning to have the desired effect!

Enjoy

Howard Marks

Howard Marks

The last honest profession

Welcome to the cannabis café... please do come in and make yourself comfortable. I would like to take you on a journey into the cooking, growing, healing and eating of this old and beautiful plant. Inside you will be treated to food for your eyes and belly, topped with a little inspiration for your mind.

At the time of writing and producing this book it is still against the law to grow or sell quantities of cannabis in the United Kingdom. This has made its completion even more challenging. Everywhere you go you will find people who love cannabis and it is on that found trust and friendship that these pages can now be shared with you.

Friends of my previous books, *Cooking with Ganja* and *Cannabis for Lunch*, will see some of their old favourites that are now complimented with a whole variety of new recipes. Every recipe is guaranteed to have been tried and tested at Eric's Kitchen. So it is with great pleasure that I am able to bring you this treasured collection.

A sprig of weed

Looking back

My work started one summer's day in the mid-eighties after I was given a handful of tiny pinhead-sized seeds that had been carefully brought back by a friend returning from India. We had grown a few plants in the past, but until

Waiting for something, Eric?

then we had always used seeds that had been found in purchased weed, mostly bought in Holland. They had all been at least three times the size of their Indian cousins.

We were not expecting much but how wrong we were. There were more plants than we thought we had seeds. The house, a two-up and two-down, was full of trays bursting with seedlings. We had planted them en masse and now we had to invest in pots and compost like there was no tomorrow.

A long summer and the use of some local fields produced a better crop than we could have ever imagined, with plentiful buds full of tight crystal clusters. During this rather heady year we built up a mountain of leftover trimmed leaf which nobody wanted to smoke, and it reached a point that whole rooms of the house were now bursting full of stuffed sacks oozing out an intoxicating rich sweet smell, not unlike that of ripening bananas left out to dry in the midday sun.

As a cook by trade I had, in the past, made the odd batch of brownies and witnessed the popularity that a bit of hash fudge had at festivals. So off I went looking for cookbooks. All I could find then was a 1973 American book called *The Art and Science of Cannabis Cookery* by Adam Gottlieb. As a result I soon married my favourite pastimes together and precipitated the beginnings of Eric's Kitchen.

Named after our rather overweight cat at the time, who now resides in a very up-market kitchen in Bath, food production began. Gladly there has never been a shortage of guests willing to try out our varied menu!

It's a new day

Open house

So, after many hours spent socialising over a hot stove, the first book was written by 1994, all I then had to do was find someone who could remove the mistakes and print it.

With the first 100 copies of *Cooking with Ganja* produced in the back room of a then seaside health food shop, there was great excitement when Alchemy, London's oldest head shop, bought their first few copies.

The next step was Glastonbury festival, which saw the first public sales of what were then rather crudely stapled together booklets. Eventually I meet Mr Gotto of Counter Culture, and it is with his guidance that *Cooking with Ganja* became a paperback and made it on to the bookshop shelves in 1997. That took us back to Glastonbury festival again where a fly pitch next to our dear friend Mr Howard Marks ensured the beginning of our first stall and its continuing popularity. We still do enjoy the festival, and the opportunity it brings to meet the many friends that all those thousands of copies sold bring to us.

It soon became apparent that there was a real need for a therapeutic guide to cannabis cookery. So, with some help from Clair Hodges of the Alliance for Cannabis Therapeutics, a second book called *Cannabis for Lunch* was created. It was particularly for people who were unwell and wanted to try cannabis possibly for the first time. The book received such a warm response that all the recipes in the Café as well as those in this book use an easy-to-follow guide with therapeutic measurements marked in green.

This book is the culmination of everything we have learned since the arrival of those tiny seeds from India nearly 20 years ago. I hope these recipes will delight the experienced cannabis cook, guide the inquisitive novice and bring relief to readers who need it.

The history of cannabis cookery

Cannabis has been used in food and drink for thousands of years. Recipes have been handed down throughout the world, many by word of mouth. Recipes were often known in rhyme for their easy recollection. One of these recipes is for Bhang (a milk drink) that dates back to 800 B.C. when it was first made in India.

It was used then and still is now as a general household remedy. There are records from China that date as far back as the 7th Century B.C. that show how hemp seed has long been used as a staple food source both for animals and for people. The seeds were gathered for their exceptional nutritional value, each one full of protein and nutrients.

Stoned again!

The flowering tops, which seem to have so wrongly brought the whole plant into conflict with some people over the years, are equally recognised and treasured for their medicinal benefits. As is the love of its use by the recreational masses. There is a great satisfaction in growing your own best quality plants packed with all the goodness of THC (Tetrahydrocannabinol), this being the naughtiest of the recognised chemicals of the 60 or so found in the plants and the one that likes to get you high. Whereas CBD (cannabidiol) is now known as the one that chills you out and is formed as the plant dries and begins to decompose.

Hemp plants only contain a very tiny amount of THC, this is why they are regarded and used differently. What determines the amount of THC in your plants is the quality of your original seed stock and the growing conditions in which you bring them up.

The taste of cannabis cookery

So, why a book on cannabis cookery, when you could just add the buds or leaves to anything, I hear you say. We tried that and soon found that cannabis does not go with everything. Its strong flavour is not always very palatable. Also different types of food need different amounts and textures of cannabis so that they blend in correctly. As a rule, cannabis does not go well with white foods, as they are often bland or delicate in flavour and do not compliment cannabis well at all. Most importantly, the effective THC needs to be treated with care. It does not dissolve in water, only in fats, alcohol and sugar. Certain types of cooking will kill the THC altogether, so if it is not prepared and cooked properly then most of it becomes a wasted product.

The cooked and eaten cannabis effect will be far more intense and last for longer than the smoked equivalent. There is not the wastage of a burning joint so you do not need to eat as much as you smoke.

All the recipes use the cannabis plants after they have been dried. The recipes call for either cannabis resin, leaf or bud, whichever is the most suitable. Damp and wet weed soon starts to go mouldy so hang it in a nice airy warm room to dry out thoroughly before you start cooking.

Cannabutter

"A little warms the heart too much burns the soul"

From *Platina (Bartholomaeus)*

This quotation is taken from what is thought to be the oldest cookbook ever written. Called *Platina (Bartholomaeus)* it was printed in 1475 and contained instructions on food preparation for around 300 recipes, one of which was for cannabis. Originally written in medieval Latin, when loosely translated into English, it gives us this first incredible piece of knowledge.

The oldest recorded cannabis recipe

De Canabi.

Eritur ' canabis ipra ut linuz:wcozticata poft

Vindemiam funeded vfum pzeftat.Awnt

canabis in alabandica ferulaY vicem in plagaY vfuz

pzebere:adeo magna in regione naicitur.

Ex remi.ne canabis tufo

ciboria queda` fi`ut:que ' ftomacto ' capiti:ac Deniqz membzis omnib9 plurim`u noc`et.

Translation

To make cannabis yourself known as flax for thread

Use a mallet to crush clods collect after good harvest

Taken as food in wine or cake

Add Cannabis to nard oil in an iron pot

Crush together over some heat until juice

A health drink of cannabis nectar

Carefully treat food and divide for the stomach and the head

finally remember everything in excess may be harmful or criminal.

Glad to know they experienced a bit of paranoia in those days too!

From medieval wine...

This is an old recipe, consumed a long time ago. If you want to recreate a real medieval banquet, bring along a rambling crowd, long tables, a wild looking dog, and some buxom wenches. No cutlery needed. Let the evening begin.

You will need

1 litre of good red wine ● a few chunks of ginger ● a few sticks of cinnamon ● a pinch of paradise, 6g (¼ oz) ground buds 3g (⅛ oz) **or use ground leaves 28g (1oz)** 14g (½ oz) **● add a cut up orange and a little honey to taste**

Method

Place all the ingredients in a large cauldron, gently warm through for an hour or so, stirring occasionally. Then strain and serve, or just drink it with the bits still in.

Known side effects include a lot of mess and some loud snoring...

Better to be choked by English hemp than poisoned by Indian Tobacco – 1602...

...to a modern day majoon

If you are on the lookout for original recipes, you will find in Jack Herers well-known book *The Emperor Wears No Clothes*, a wonderful advert for the very popular Hashish Candy sold across America in the late 1800s and early 1900s by the Ganjah Wallah Co.

In these candy bars finely ground hashish was added to a rich maple syrup in what was regarded as a real family favourite with adverts recommending it as a 'complete mental and physical invigorator' at 25 cents each or $1 per box. You can find our version of the recipe on page 132.

Another of my favourite cooks is a lady called Alice B. Toklas who had a cannabis brownie recipe in the 1954 edition of her cookbook censored. Not one to give up she later became well known for her version of hashish majoon (a type of truffle) originally an Islamic delicacy which we have also included on page 26. The recipe was printed in several later editions of what was otherwise a very traditional cookbook. A perfect mixture of fruit, spices, nuts and butter with the suggested addition of a bunch of cannabis sativa. This was an inspiration to the many cooks and their books that followed her. Eric's Kitchen will now take you into the 21st Century with the widest selection of mind blowing sweets, puddings and full course dinners all made for you to enjoy.

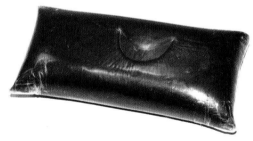

A 9oz-bar of soap (Moroccan)

Taking it easy before you start

Each recipe has been fully tested so we can offer portion guides to show how many people will get stoned with the amount of cannabis used in each recipe.

If you have not eaten cannabis before, you may like to start with smaller amounts than suggested. Even if you smoke cannabis regularly its effect when eaten is intensified and will last a lot longer than if you had smoked it.

If you should feel unwell – lay down in a quiet place and try to sleep it off. The worst thing that can happen to you is that you will experience nausea and vomit. If this does happen just remember that no one has ever been recorded as dying from eating cannabis, so there is no need to panic.

If you are going to add cannabis to a large meal then all those little leaf clippings are ideal. Remember you will not get the best effects if you eat your top grade cannabis mixed in with large amounts of food. (This is because the THC is absorbed by the liver when you eat it which turns it into eleven-hydroxy THC. In this form it takes longer for you to feel the effects). Alcohol and sugar in small food amounts both speed up the absorption of THC into the blood stream.

The therapeutic guide is given in green throughout the book which shows how much to use if your desire is not to become intoxicated, but rather to assist in treatment. Generally this is half the amount given for recreational use.

All of the measurements are based on good average stock, not super strength. Sometimes your cannabis may be weaker – therefore you will need to add a little more than suggested. You will soon get to know what suits you as you begin to experiment with different types of cannabis and different recipes.

Once you have prepared your cannabis in any form do not leave it exposed for long periods, as it will begin to lose some of its potency.

Pollen hashish

The basic preparations

Hashish: Comes in many different colours and textures. This solid form of cannabis is made from the plants most potent flowering tops, with its colours varying from a light caramel brown to reddish golden creams through to deep dark brown and black, sometimes with a tint of the darkest olive green.

The texture of hash can be soft and oily while others vary from light and crumbly, to rock hard. To test the quality warm slightly and smell, if it bubbles or smells unnatural don't use it. It should have an earthy or a pungent sweetness about it. Warmed gently in a small metal bowl and crumbled to a fine powder, it gives the appearance of other common ground spices, and it's ready for cooking.

Sacred Ghee preparation

Hashish blocks are often named after their country or village of origin. Here are some well known ones: Moroccan, Black, Gold Seal, Lebanese, Afghani, Nepalese, Rose of Lebanon. ● **Bombay Black:** Low-grade Indian blended hashish mix. ● **Charis:** Plant resin made and collected by hand, a techinique known as rubbing. An age old method of breaking down the clear resin glands (Trichome) to produce beautiful soft black oily balls (such as Nepalese temple balls) or squashed flat into soft patties. ● **Gomma:** The term for hand-rubbed hashish made in Morocco. ● **Hooch:** An Australian name for cannabis. ● **Cream:** Top quality hash made from the sticky Trichomes alone. ● **Skuff:** Top grade Dutch hash made from loaded skunk buds. ● **Kif:** The Moroccan word for cannabis. ● **Ice Hash:** Made by being passed through ice to collect all the Trichomes; it is good quality but also very sticky and not so easy to cook with. ● **Nederhash:** A respectable home-made Dutch hashish.

Buds: These are the strongest most sought after part of the female plant which form clusters on each branch. It is best to use them once they are properly dry; try not to handle them too much. Hold the plant by the stalk and snip finely with a good pair of scissors over a clean bowl so you're sure to catch all those wonderful crystals. Or alternatively, get a weed grinder, an excellent little addition to your kitchen tools. ● **Fresh Leaves:** Rinse the leaves and bring to the boil in water, strain and grind with a little milk to make Bhang paste. The water will not absorb the essential properties from the leaves. ● **Dry Leaves:** To obtain dry leaves hang them in a warm place to dry out, then remove stalks and grind leaves to a fine powder, this is often called Hemp or Leaf Flour. ● **Seeds:** Nutty in flavour, soaked in water and ground to a pulp which can be added to other foods or made into a natural health drink. ● **Hash Oil:** Use in very small amounts and respect its strength! It is often regarded as a Class A drug and often carries heavier penalties. ● **Hemp Oil:** Only contains trace THC, made from the seeds it is a healthy alternative, although because of its richness it should be used sparingly. It is not suitable for deep-fat, high-heat cooking.

Freshly ground

Cannabutter

You will need

450g (1lb) butter ● 25g (1oz) good buds or hashish 14g (½ oz) or 50g (2oz) ground leaves 25g (1oz)

Method

Melt the butter slowly in a pan. Grind down your weed to a fine powder and sift out any stalks. Gently add to the melted butter and stir in well. It will turn into a wonderful dark emerald green. If you are using hashish, warm it in a small pan or spoon over a very low heat, or gently warm in the microwave for 5-10 seconds on medium not full power, until you can crumble it away with your fingers ready to add to the butter.

Keep on a low heat for up to half an hour without letting it burn, whilst giving it plenty of stirring.

Then pour through a fine strainer squeezing all the butter into a jug.

You can use the mush in a drink or simply compost it. Pour your Cannabutter into jars and seal them tightly for storage in the fridge. If you cover the hardened butter with a little water, this will help it keep a little longer. For general use, 1 teaspoon per person should be enough to start with.

Before you use any of the cannabutter you can add lots of other flavours to give it a better taste. Why not try ½-1 teaspoons of Dijon mustard or pesto sauce, which makes it ideal to use in savoury cooking, or you can use a mixture of herbs such as thyme, rosemary, oregano and chives.

For sweet cooking mix in ½ tablespoon of finely grated orange and lemon peel with ½ tablespoon of juice or add ¼ teaspoon of mixed spice. For coffee butter simply add ½ tablespoon of strong black coffee and mix in well.

Ounce weights				
Butter: 450g (16oz)	220g (8oz)	100g (4oz)	50g (2oz)	25g (1oz)
Ganja: 25g (1oz)	14g (½ oz)	7g (¼ oz)	3.5g (⅛ oz)	1.75g (1/16 oz)

Sacred ghee

You will need

450g (1lb) of butter ● 25g (1oz) good buds or hashish 14g (½ oz) or 50g (2oz) leaves 25g (1oz)

Method

Using this traditional method will stop the butter from going rancid even if you don't have a fridge to store it in. It will also have a nice nutty, butterscotch flavour.

Heat the butter slowly in a pan. Bring it to the boil and remove the froth from the top and discard it. Carry on until it stops frothing.

Your ghee is now ready for you to add the ganja using the same amounts as with cannabutter.

If using hashish, firstly heat it in a metal bowl or on a large spoon over a low heat. When it is warmed through it should crumble easily into a fine powder. You will also find that hash dissolves quicker than grass. Stir the cannabis well into the ghee on a low heat for about 15 minutes, then strain and store in air tight clean jars.

Once you have made the ghee you can use it in a lot of the following recipes to replace some or all of the butter needed or simply add to your own favourites. For general use, 1 teaspoon per person to start with.

Melting together

Bhang paste

You will need

225g (¹⁄₂ lb) seeds ground ● 2-3g (¹⁄₈ oz) ground grass ● a little milk or use a tablespoon of hemp oil ● 1-2g (¹⁄₁₆ oz) cannabis

Method

Made easily by using well ground seeds and adding ground grass and a little milk to make this excellent cooking paste. Or simply grind your grass directly with a little milk.

If you are using hemp oil, warm it for 5 minutes with the powdered hash to make a potent mix ready for cooking.

If cannabis is boiled or over cooked it will destroy the THC. With gentle cooking, the fats will absorb it all, which can only improve on the strength and flavour increasing its overall effect.

You can also add lecithin, which is found naturally in both cow and soya milk. This can be bought in powdered form from health food shops, and works as an emulsifier helping to evenly absorb and distribute the fats, which have absorbed the THC. You can add between 3-4 teaspoons to a recipe.It is very useful in soups and dressings where the oil tends to separate, or in dishes with little fat content.

Grind...

Grind...

Paste

Indian bhang

You will need

3g (¹⁄₈ oz) butter ● 2 cups of
milk, any sort ● 1-2g of hash or
grass ● a pinch of spice

Method

Melt the butter in a pan, add
powdered cannabis and simmer for
one minute, then pour in the milk
and warm gently. Add spices,
cinnamon and nutmeg are good,
you may also like to add some
honey to taste.

If you want to give it a real kick,
add some vodka!

Pita pata pita pata

Hash oil honey

You will need

1 tablespoon of ghee or butter ● **¹/₂ cup of runny honey** ● **1 gram of hash oil**

Method

Hash oil comes in different refinements, from brown oil (being its crudest), to red amber, honey and white oil (being the best).

Heat the ghee or butter in a small pan then add the honey and oil and stir in well over a low heat for 5 minutes then pour into jars and allow to cool before putting the lids on.

¹/₂ -1 teaspoon should be sufficient per person. It is nice on toast or in a cup of hot water for that good morning cup of hash oil tea.

Hash oil is hard to come by and can be up to four times stronger than the hash it was made from.

This means it is highly concentrated and it should be used with respect.

Honey

Majoon

This is an Arabic word for cannabis confections so you may find sweet and savoury recipes with this name often with regional differences which depend on what was available to the cook. They all contain fat or oil of some sort and care should be taken not to overcook and burn them. They are often regarded as aphrodisiacs in Arabic medicine.

Makes about 20

Eat 1-2 each

You will need

14g (½ oz) butter ● 7g (¼ oz) well ground good buds 3g (⅛ oz) ● 50g (2oz) washed and chopped dates and figs ● 25g (1oz) chopped nuts ● 1 tablespoon honey ● 1 teaspoon of each spice ginger, nutmeg and cinnamon

Method

Warm butter, add weed and all other ingredients and cook on a gentle heat, for 10-12 minutes stirring occasionally. Pour into a greased backing tray and allow to cool, then cut into small squares or roll into balls and serve with natural yoghurt.

This type of recipe is commonly found in many cultures, often as a medicinal cure for pain.

Before the arrival of tobacco, hashish was most commonly eaten. In Morocco this tradition is still reserved in a sweet *maaju`n* made from a simple bhang paste cut into small easy-to-eat tablet-size pieces. They are taken on the tongue and washed down with a glass of hot sweet mint tea. It is, however, not possible to buy them, as they are a delicacy that are served to welcome guests, to eat at the end of a special meal.

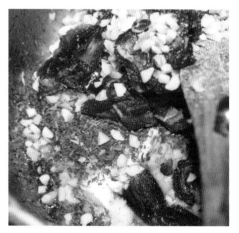

Mixing together

Bits and pieces

Cannabis indica: A small plant originating from the Hindu-Kush area of central Asia, ideal for outdoor use in cooler climates. ● **Cannabis sativa:** Tall plants that like it hot and steamy, producing a jazzy high with a fruity smell. ● **Cannabis ruderalis:** This plant is strong and hardy and can be found wild in parts of Russia. ● **Ganja:** An Indian word that covers the whole plant. Wild ganja is known as jungi. ● **Grass or weed:** Can mean the plant form either fresh or dried. ● **Hash oil:** A highly potent semi liquid, which can be dangerous to extract and consume in quantity. ● **Hemp plant:** Contains very low THC and does not get you stoned. ● **Hemp oil:** A nutritional and versatile oil made from the seeds. ● **Leaves**: Use dried and ground for cooking. ● **Marijuana:** An American term for cannabis plants dried flowers. ● **Sensimelia**: Un-pollinated seedless female plant known for its increased potentency ● **THC:** Tetrahydrocannabinol is the bit that gets you stoned! ● **Trichome:** Resin glands – good plants are covered in them.

Soft black hashish

"At last some good growing weather." Just what we all need. There is nothing better than picking fresh weed from the garden and spending Sunday mornings enjoying tending those big buds.

There is no doubt competition will be "high" at this year's local fair, complete with laden tables straining under the weight of cannabis foods, all delicately prepared with the finest of ingredients. As pensioners clash with teenagers in the demand to buy Farmer Jones's new strain of purple skunkweed, along with a pot of his best clotted. The supermarket shelves will soon topple with luxury pickles and olives soaked in cannabis oil. The deli counters will show off their superior soft and hard cheeses streaked with the green veins of weed. But, best of all, the bakeries will be full of tempting cakes and pastries dripping in thick, sweet ganja icing. I can feel a little shopping coming on.

It's a surprise

Eat 1-2 each

You will need

50g (2oz) butter ● 2 tablespoons cocoa ● 3 tablespoons condensed milk ● 50g (2oz) soft brown sugar ● 3g (1/8 oz) finely ground hash or good weed 2g (1/16 oz) ● 150g (6oz) desiccated coconut ● 125g (5oz) small white marshmallows

Method

Melt the butter in a pan then add the cocoa, milk, sugar and hash. Continue to heat, stirring occasionally, until it is all melted together – take care not to let it boil.

Remove from the heat and add most of the coconut, just saving a little. Divide the mixture into 15 balls and flatten each one out enough to hug around a marshmallow. Once you've done this, roll in last of the coconut.

Green straws

Makes about 40

Eat about 5 each

You will need

50g (2oz) plain flour ● 14g
(¹/₂ oz) butter ● 14g (¹/₂ oz) finely
grated cheese ● salt & pepper
(Cayenne pepper is good) ● 7g
(¹/₄ oz) ground leaves 3g (¹/₈ oz)
or 3g (¹/₈ oz) ground buds or
powdered hashish 2g (¹/₁₆ oz)
● 1 egg yolk or milk

Method

Rub the butter into the flour and add
the cheese, seasoning and cannabis.
Add a little of the egg yolk or milk to
bring the mixture to a firm dough.
Knead a little and make into straws
or any other shape of your choice.
Place on a lightly greased baking
sheet, bake for 10-12 minutes at
230°c/450°f/gas 8.

Alive

You can double the recipe for
enough pastry to make a flan,
though it is better to keep the ganja
amount the same as it tends to
become too green. This dough
freezes well.

Shish kebabs

These are easy, light summer treats you can make into great kebabs with roasted vegetables cooked in the oven and flavoured on the BBQ.

You will need

500g (1lb) minced lamb or veggie mince ● 2 tablespoons celery leaves, finely chopped ● 2 tablespoons parsley, finely chopped ● 2 tablespoons (1 tablespoon) dried and well ground leaves ● 2 onions, finely choppped ● 1 teaspoon turmeric

Method

Mix ingredients together and roll into small sausage shapes, then skewer them and cook under a medium grill for 7-8 minutes. Finish off by placing on the edge of a calm BBQ for a further 2-3 minutes. Serve with a crispy green salad.

Banana treat

While the coals are cooling take 4-6 bananas, peel, then wrap back in their skins, cover and twist in foil like giant sweets. Leave them to cook gently on the BBQ for 15-20 minutes, turning them over once or twice; unwrap and serve with cream for a real munchies treat.

Freshly picked

Caramel shoes

Makes about 20

You will need

100g (4oz) unsalted butter

- 150g (4½ oz) plain flour
- 75 g (3oz) soft brown sugar
- 3-4g (⅛ oz) finely crumbled

hashish 2g (1/16 oz)

Method

These are so easy to make!
Lightly butter a baking sheet and
heat the oven to 190°c/375°f/
gas 5.

Place all the ingredients into a
bowl and knead with your hands
to make a nice smooth dough.
Shape the dough into approximately
20 little balls and place on a
greased baking sheet. Press each
one lightly and bake for 15 minutes
or alternatively you can roll out
like pastry and cut out some
fancy shapes.

London marches on

Glastonbury mud cake

Mud has never been so good!

Makes about 12 portions
Eat 1 portion each

You will need

4 eggs separated ● 225g (8oz) caster sugar ● 170g (6oz) butter ● 225g (8oz) dark chocolate (grated) ● black hash is especially good for this cake or use fresh oily bud, finely chopped. 7g (¼oz) or 3-4g (⅛oz) ● 2 tablespoons hemp oil or a light olive oil ● 85g (3oz) self-raising flour

Method

Heat the oven to 190°c/375°f/gas 5 and grease an 8-inch (200mm) loose-based tin. Separate the eggs and beat the whites until stiff.

In another bowl beat together the egg yolks and the sugar then cream-in the butter. Add chocolate, cannabis, oil and flour. Then fold in the egg whites and pour into your tin. Bake on the middle shelf for 1½ hours. Allow to cool and cut into about 12 slices.

Hit me with that breadstick!

Eat 1-2 slices each

You will need

a clear head! ● a sharp knife (adult supervision) ● a medium bread baguette ● 100g (4oz) butter or vegan margarine ● 1 teaspoon mixed herbs ● 2 crushed garlic cloves ● 2-4g (1/8 oz) pre-ground buds would be ideal ● tin foil ● and an oven, switched on to 200˚c/400˚f/ gas 6

Method

Thickly slice the bread leaving it still holding together at the bottom of each slice.

Mix the butter, crushed garlic and all the herbs together, beating with a fork until well blended.

Butter each slice of bread on both sides, push the baguette back together and roll up in foil ready to bake for 10-15 minutes.

Enjoy!

Cosmic cookies

A favourite treat for all at Eric's Kitchen is our yearly trek to the Glastonbury festival. It's a pleasure to meet our customers and try everyone else's sweets and treats.

Always on the look out for new recipes this is where I came across these completely organic and vegan cookies, made for us by the Cosmic Cookie Co. who were kind enough to share with us this adapted old Greek recipe that they have taken from the traditional and turned into a scrumptious 21st Century treat.

Makes 18-20

Eat 1-2 each

You will need

200 ml organic light olive oil or you can use a fifty fifty mix with organic hemp oil ● 100 ml freshly squeezed orange juice

● 100 ml organic red wine

● 1 teaspoon organic cinnamon

● 1 dessert spoon grated fresh ginger ● 75g (3oz) organic vine fruits (a mix of currants and sultanas) ● a pinch of salt

● 150g (6oz) of the best organic Belgium plain chocolate

● 2 tablespoons organic dried mango (or, as we did in the latest batch, use dried cranberries, but you can always use a few more sultanas) ● 100ml maple syrup

● self-raising organic flour to mix up to 400g (14oz)

Method

Soak your ground cannabis leaves in the oil using about 14g ($^1/_2$ oz) per 200ml. Then gently warm 3-4 g ($^1/_8$ oz) of hashish or good quality buds and grind down to a smooth powder, adding to the oil. This perfect mix, is now ready to use.

Hand-made...

Put all the wet ingredients into a saucepan leaving out only the chocolate and flour. Mix and warm gently on a medium heat making sure it does not boil. Once combined and warmed through, remove from the heat and gradually sift in the flour stirring with a large wooden spoon, until the mixture forms a big soft ball. If it's too sticky allow the mixture to cool for a bit.

"Stick the kettle on for tea would you... and while you are there put the oven on to 170°c/325°f/ gas 3. Cheers."

Then using clean hands, pinch off small balls and flatten out ready to place onto a lightly greased baking sheet. "Sorry, did I not tell you to get that ready?" You could also use

tried and tested...

a teaspoon to measure out the cookie mixture, ready to flatten with the back of a spoon. Cut up the chocolate into small rough chunks and sprinkle a few pieces on each cookie. Allow them to cook for 15-20 minutes then turn and cook for another 15-20 minutes. Remove from the oven and allow to cool on a rack, try one – they are delicious just what you need to go with that cup of....

"Have you not made that tea yet?"

...and very effective!

Black hash fudge

Makes about 60 pieces
Eat 2-3 each

You will need

125g (4oz) butter ● 125g
(4oz) chocolate (broken into
pieces) ● 340g (12oz) icing
sugar ● 2 tablespoons of milk
● 125g (4oz) crushed pecan nuts
● 7g (¼ oz) finely crumbled
hashish 3-4g (⅛ oz)

Method

Take a large baking tray and rub
over with some soft butter, then
cover with a piece of foil and rub it
over again to give a thin covering
of soft butter. Using a heavy-based
saucepan put in everything except
the hash and nuts. Stir over a low
heat until everything has melted
together and the mixture begins
to boil.

Remove from the heat and
add your prepared hash and
nuts then give it a good beating.
Pour into the tin, smoothing
it over to about 1cm deep.
Then allow to cool before cutting
into squares. This will make
plenty for a party or it will keep
in a tin for about a week.

Sweet shop dreams...

Something's cooking!

Maple and pecan ice cream

Eat 1 scoop each

You will need

1 1/2 litres (2 pints) of ready-made custard ● 3 tablespoons maple syrup ● 280ml (10fl oz) double cream ● 100g (4oz) of well chopped pecans or you could use walnuts ● 3g (1/8 oz) finely powdered light hash pollen is ideal 2g (1/16 oz)

Method

Line a shallow rectangular baking tray with cling film allowing it to drape over the sides. In a large bowl mix together the custard and maple syrup. In a separate bowl whisk the cream until thick and then fold into the custard followed by the nuts and hash, making sure they are well distributed throughout. Freeze overnight in a plastic tub. (Wait until the surface is firm before putting the lid on.) Remove from the freezer and allow to stand and soften before serving with a swizzle of maple syrup.

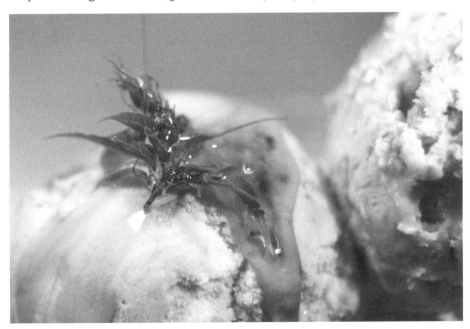

Naughty!

Sticky weed and toffee sauce

Stop dribbling!

You will need

50g (2oz) butter ● 75g (3oz) soft brown sugar ● 2 tablespoons of double or single cream ● ½-1 teaspoon of ground weed (or some light fluffy pollen flowers)

Method

Melt the butter, sugar and cream into a pan and bring to the boil for 2 minutes. Remove from the heat and sprinkle on your weed, stirring gently for a few more minutes as the mix begins to cool. Pour over ice cream.

Anyone for tea?

You will need

1-2 grams of good hash to each

- **1 fluid ounce alcohol (vodka)**
- **a pot of tea**

Method

THC is not soluble in water, so the steeping of leaves to make a tea produces flavour but will have no effect. However, add a teaspoon of Hash oil honey (see page 25) to the boiling water and it's a different story. Alternatively, you can use a shot of vodka in your tea. By gently heating the vodka and stirring in your hash until it dissolves then add to a pot of regular tea.

In Jamaica, weed tea is often served with a little added condensed milk, which also works to absorb the THC. However, it is extremely sweet.

You can also add this mixture of alcohol and cannabis to a bottle of wine by removing the equivalent amount of wine to that of prepared vodka and cannabis and drinking it. Pour the hot vodka mixture back in

Or would you care for something a little stronger?

and re-cork the bottle. Shake well and save for a rainy day. Label the bottle clearly, remember your wine will be more alcoholic with the vodka added.

Truffle rhyme

The reason I love truffles
They get me off my head
I love the creeping death
And the way my eyes turn red

When you eat these truffles
You soon may seem confused
Your legs will go all wobbly
The mind numb and bemused

The magic of these truffles
They're not only for fun,
They have more serious uses
Medical tests are being run

Some people eat these truffles
To help them ease the pain
The doctors can't prescribe it,
These laws are quite insane

The best thing about these truffles
And it's the last thing I shall say
Eat a few of these, and
You will have a peaceful day

By Tom

High times

Drunken truffles

This is the easiest way I have found yet to make a good truffle. They keep for weeks in an airtight container in the fridge.

Eat 1-2 each

You will need
225g (8oz) good chocolate
● 1 tablespoon (15ml) condensed milk ● 14g (¹/₂ oz) ground dried leaves 7g (¹/₄ oz) or 3-4g (¹/₈ oz) hash or good buds 2g (¹/₁₆ oz) ● 1 capful of your favourite spirit, liqueur or sweet wine ● cocoa for dusting

Taking the struggle out of making a truffle!

Method
Melt the chocolate in a bowl over hot water (not boiling).

Then add the condensed milk, prepared cannabis and booze. Remove from the heat, beat well, and leave to cool for a few minutes.

Wash hands and dust in cocoa powder, ready to roll mixture into truffle balls. Makes around 20 truffles in less than 10 minutes. Eaten in five!

Savour that moment

Eric cooks for Howard – one of his favourite dishes...
Savoury bread and butted pud

Serves 4-6

You will need

40g (1-1½ oz) of soft butter

- 1 leek, washed and chopped
- 1 small red onion, chopped
- 1 small or half a pepper, sliced
- 8-10 slices of bread cut into half triangles (it's OK to use bread that's going stale) ● 100g (4oz) chunky ham chopped up
- 4g (⅛ oz) of well-ground buds 2g (1/16 oz) ● 150g (5oz) good cheddar or tasty cheese ● 1 pint milk ● 3 eggs ● salt & freshly ground pepper to taste

Method

Set the oven to 190°c/375°f/gas 5 and lightly butter a 2-pint oven dish. In a pan melt the remaining butter and sweat the leek, onion and pepper for a few minutes.

Now layer half of the bread into the dish and cover with the onion and pepper mix, then sprinkle with half of your ham and cheese followed by an even dusting of all the ground weed. Then layer with the last of the bread and again with the ham and cheese. Beat together your eggs and milk season and pour over the dish.

Allow it to soak in for several minutes before baking for about half an hour.

Bread

Butted

Mr Nice and easy cake

Serves 8-10

You will need

285g (10oz) caster sugar
● 170g (6oz) margarine or
butter ● 14g (½ oz) ground
leaves 7g (¼ oz) or 3-4 g (⅛ oz)
hash or good buds 2g (¹⁄₁₆ oz)
● 3 eggs ● 1 teaspoon vanilla
essence ● 170g (6oz) fromage
frais ● 225g (8oz) self-raising
flour ● 50g (2oz) cocoa ● 50g
(2oz) dark chocolate (grated)
● 1 teaspoon bicarbonate of soda

Method

Heat the oven to 170°c/325°f/
gas 3.

Grease a 9-inch (225mm) cake
tin and dust with flour. Beat together
the sugar, butter and cannabis.
Fold in the eggs, vanilla essence,
and fromage frais. Stir in the cocoa,
chocolate, flour and bicarbonate
of soda then mix until smooth.
Pour the mixture into the cake tin
and bake for 40-45 minutes. This is
one mixing bowl you won't want the
children to lick clean! Test with a
skewer, if it comes out clean, the
cake is ready. Cool on a wire rack
and cover in thick icing or cream.

Have a nice time!

"That was a 9-inch tin, or was it centimetres?... whoops"!

The beauty of a fresh autumn morning starts with an early walk that could lead anywhere. We take a left down a little lane almost hidden by twisted knotted trees and covered in hanging ivy. The lane soon becomes just a dusty old stone track, its sides densely overhung with cowslips and wild poppies. Leading us deep into a thick wooded area, where the morning's mist can still be seen clinging to the trees, the path weaves itself through like a snake until it comes to a natural end. We step into the light of day and before us stands the most amazing and magnificent sight of row upon row of cannabis plants, each one waving gently in the soft breeze. And not a male to be seen!

Our senses are overcome, faced with such a vast quantity of weed but we quickly recover and start to fill our baskets, picking the most laden buds we can find.

Our hands black and dripping with oil, the baskets bulging under the weight, we turn and head back down the long narrow row of plants, their scent so pungent that it is becoming intoxicating. We run recklessly to reach the woods gasping for fresh air. The path seems faster on the way back and we are soon stumbling in through the kitchen door.

Something for lunch

This is a great way of eating some of those good for you hemp seeds with some of that fresh weed. Always make two, one without the weed for the munchies later. Seed and weed.

Fancy a salad?

Makes about 8-10

Eat 1-2 each

leaves 3-4g (⅛ oz) or 3g (⅛ oz) of ground buds 2g (¹⁄₁₆ oz)

You will need

110g (4oz) butter ● 110g (4oz) rolled oats ● 110g (4oz) hemp seeds (soaked for 10 minutes and washed) ● 110g (4oz) grated cheese ● a small amount of grated onion, if desired ● ½ teaspoon mustard powder ● salt & pepper ● 1 egg ● 7g (¼ oz) ground

Method

Heat your oven to 200°c/400°f/ gas 6. Soften the butter, grind the weed and add everything together. Mix well, press into a greased tin and cook for 30 minutes. Cool and cut into squares, ready to serve with a tomato and fresh leaf salad. "They are delicious!"

Sweet bread and butter for pudding

This is easy to make and is good to use up bread that's started to go stale. You can also use currant buns, fruit bread and even slices of malt loaf.

You will need

8-10 slices of stale bread ● 40g (1½ oz) butter ● apricot jam ● 50g (2oz) sultanas or raisins ● 25g (1oz) chopped apricot ● 25g (1oz) washed and chopped cherries or papaya ● 2 tablespoons ground buds or 1 tablespoon ● 3 eggs ● ½ pint (280ml) milk ● a pinch of nutmeg ● 50g (2oz) brown sugar

Really fruity!

Method

Set the oven to 180°c/350°f/gas 4 and lightly grease a large 2-pint oven dish.

Then butter and jam each slice of bread and cut into triangles. Layer half the bread into the dish then sprinkle with half the fruit and ground weed. Repeat with a layer of the remaining bread and top with the rest of the fruit.

Beat the eggs and milk together, add the nutmeg and sugar and pour over the dish allowing it to soak in for a while before baking for about half an hour.

Lovely served with custard and or fresh cream.

Any cheese pasties

Makes 6-8 pasties

You will need

200g (8oz) new potatoes ● 100g
(4oz) well-chopped turnip, onion
and a small carrot ● 450g (1lb)
minced beef, lamb or turkey
(use a veggie mix if you prefer)
● 100g (4oz) your favourite
cheese from the board, diced
● a good pinch of mixed herbs
● a little oil ● 7g (¼ oz) finely
chopped leaves 3-4g (⅛ oz)
● 3g (⅛ oz) good buds 2g (¹⁄₁₆ oz)
● 675g (1½ lb) shortcrust pastry

Pick any cheese!

Method

Set the oven to 200°c/400°f/
gas 6.

Prepare your vegetables and
bring to the boil to soften. Toss the
meat in some hot oil to seal it and
then combine all the filling
ingredients into a bowl with plenty
of seasoning.

Roll out the pastry and using a
small plate cut out 6-8 rounds.
Spoon one tablespoon of the meat
and vegetable mix into the centre
of each round. Brush the edges
with a little milk and fold up the
sides, pinching them together with
your fingers. Place onto a lightly
floured baking sheet and brush
each of the pasties with a thin coat
of milk.

Bake for 20 minutes on the
middle shelf. Then cover in foil,
lower the heat to 180°c/350°f/
gas 4, and bake for another 30
minutes – this will stop them
browning too much.

Mellow browns

Eat 1 at a time!

You will need

170g (6 oz) butter ● 2 tablespoons cocoa ● 14g (¹/₂ oz) ground leaves 7g (¹/₄ oz) or 3-4g (¹/₈ oz) hash or good buds 2g (¹/₁₆ oz) ● 170g (6oz) caster sugar ● 2 eggs ● 50g (2oz) chopped walnuts or pecan nuts ● 50g (2oz) plain flour ● 85g (3oz) mini marshmallows ● 85g (3oz) chocolate chips

Method

Melt 50g (2oz) of butter in a pan or you can simply melt 50g (2oz) of cannabutter (see page 21) if you have some made. Add the cocoa and mix until smooth. Then stir in the finely ground cannabis, and set aside to cool.

Cream together the remaining butter and sugar, beat in the eggs, and then add the cocoa and cannabis mixture then gradually fold in the walnuts and flour.

Turn into a 7-inch square greased baking tin (not you, the mixture)

and bake at 180°c/350°f/gas 4 for 30 to 35 minutes

Remove from the oven, sprinkle the marshmallows and chocolate chips evenly on the top and add a few crushed nuts if you have any left over.

Return to the oven for 2-3 minutes then remove and allow to cool before cutting.

Stir in the hashish

Decorate the top

Peanut butter cookies

Makes 20-25 cookies

Eat 1-2 each

You will need

100g (4oz) butter ● ½ teaspoon grated lemon rind ● 14g (½ oz) ground leaves 7g (¼ oz) or 3-4g (⅛ oz) ground hash or good buds 2g (1/16 oz) ● 100g (4oz) peanut butter (I didn't forget it this time!) ● 85g (3oz) sugar ● 85g (3oz) brown sugar ● 140g (5oz) plain flour ● 1 teaspoon bicarbonate of soda ● a pinch salt ● 7g (¼ oz) whole unsalted peanuts

Method

If you are using your ready-made cannabutter (see page 21) then use 25g (1oz) of that to 75g (3oz) plain butter.

Cream together the butter, lemon rind, prepared cannabis, peanut butter, and all the sugar. Then sift in the flour, soda and salt and fold

Cookie stack

into mixture. Turn on to a flour dusted board.

Dust your hands with flour, or the mixture will stick to you like mad, and roll into approximately 20 small balls.

Place on a greased oven sheet and press down with the back of a fork, sprinkle with nuts. Bake for 15 minutes on the middle shelf at about 180°c/350°f/gas 4.

Allow to cool for a few minutes before removing onto a wire rack. Try to leave to cool a little more before eating, that's the hardest part!

International feta parcels

Personally recommended by Sue Arnold in her column (*Independent on Saturday*) as a wonderful treat and very good for your eyesight too!

Serves 6-8 people

You will need

25g (1oz) melted butter
- 1 large onion, chopped
- 25g (1oz) ground leaves

14g (1/2 oz) or 7g (1/4 oz) of best buds 3g (1/8 oz) • 500g (1lb) of frozen chopped spinach, defrosted and drained • 225g (8oz) feta or ricotta cheese • 2 bunches spring onions, chopped • 25g (1oz) parsley or basil, chopped • salt & pepper • 10 sheets of filo pastry (or you can use a block of defrosted puff pastry)

Method

Melt the butter and fry the onions for five minutes. Add the ground leaf or bud and stir in well, keeping on a low heat for a few minutes. Meanwhile, put the spinach in a bowl, crumble in the cheese, then add the cooked onions and herbs; mix well. Lay the pastry sheets

Light to eat...

...knocks you off your feet!

onto a flat surface and brush with melted butter.

Add a little of the mixture to each and gather the pastry up to make little parcels.

Then bake for 20-25 minutes at 180°c/350°f/gas 4. If using puff pastry, roll out cut into squares and repeat the same process. Ready to serve with a little sweet and sour sauce and salad.

Green sea soup

Adapted from an old 17th Century recipe one that has been served and very much enjoyed at many a laden table.

Fancy a swim?

Serves 10

You will need

100g (4oz) butter ● 500g (1lb) frozen or fresh peas ● 2 leeks, chopped ● 2 cloves of garlic ● 50g (2oz) diced bacon ● 3 pints of chicken stock ● 50g (2oz) of spinach, fresh or frozen ● 50g (2oz) white cabbage, finely chopped ● ½ a lettuce, chopped ● a handful of parsley ● 2 celery stalks, chopped ● 1 punnet of mustard and cress, chopped ● 1 branch of mint, chopped ● 50g (2oz) fresh or dried weed leaves 28g (1oz)

Method

Gently sauté the peas, leeks, garlic and bacon in half the butter until soft. Add the stock and simmer for 20 minutes. Then liquidize.

Melt the remaining butter and layer in the spinach, cabbage, lettuce, parsley, celery, mustard and cress, mint and weed. Allow to gently cook for about 20 minutes until soft then add the pureed pea mix. Stir and season to taste. Serve with thick, buttered granary bread or croutons.

Stink-pot

It's easy to do and serves 2!

You will need

1-2 grams dried bud ● 300ml (1/2-pint) milk ● 2 teaspoons of drinking chocolate ● 2 dollops of cream, if required

Method

In a clean bowl gently rub some of your dried bud with your fingertips to catch some the crystals and hairs, and set this aside. Then using the grinder (you should have one by now) grind the buds as fine as you can.

Simply fill two cups with milk (full fat is best) pour into a pan and warm through. Add the fine bud and stir on a gentle heat – do not boil.

Pour back into the cups and add a teaspoon of drinking chocolate, in each and top with a squirt of cream, which will add a little more fat to help absorb that all important THC.

Northern lights

You can add sugar if required as this also helps to give quicker absorption of the effective THC into the blood stream. This rapidly produces an overwhelming desire to smile and to want to join the dog for its afternoon nap.

Don't forget to sprinkle with the crystals you have saved.

Cappuccino toast

Let yourself be seduced by our bedtime snack.

Eat 1 slice each

You will need

85g (3oz) grated dark or milk chocolate ● 25g (1oz) soft butter ● 1 teaspoon of strong black coffee ● 1-2 g finely powdered sticky hash ● 4 slices of fruit or chocolate bread (ask at your bakery)

Method

Grate the chocolate or shave bits off with a knife. Then beat the warmed and powdered hash into the butter with the coffee.

Combine well and spread over each slice of chocolate bread. Sprinkle with the grated chocolate and sandwich with the remaining two slices then toast on both sides.

Chocolate bread

Sleep well!

An indica-sativa cross

Vegetarian and vegan alternatives

A lot of our recipes can easily be altered to suit the vegetarian or vegan diet by using alternative ingredients.

Agar Agar: This is derived from seaweed, can be used instead of gelatine. ● **Carob:** (A chocolate alternative) contains no caffeine and bars can be melted like any other chocolate. ● **Tahini:** Mixed with maple syrup makes a surprisingly good cream alternative. ● **Soya:** Among the huge variety of soya products available, there can be found alternatives for margarine, milk, cream and yoghurt. ● **Oil and flour:** When blended these two can be used as a substitute for a binding egg (as in the Vegan cake recipe opposite). ● **TVP:** A textured vegetable protein which can be used as an alternative to meat. It can be bought in chunks or as mince. ● **Tofu:** This is a soya beancurd full of protein frequently used in vegetarian dishes. It can be a little bland in taste and requires some strong flavours to make it more tasty. It can be used in both sweet and savoury dishes.

Unmeasured

Your vegan cake sir...

You will need

a little vegan margarine for greasing ● 275g (10oz) self-raising flour ● 50g (2oz) cocoa ● 3 teaspoons baking powder ● 255g (9oz) caster sugar ● 1 teaspoon vanilla extract ● 9 tablespoons hemp or sunflower oil ● 320ml (12fl oz) water ● 14g (1/2 oz) ground leaves 7g (1/4 oz) or 3-4g (1/8 oz) hash or good buds 2g (1/16 oz)

For the filling & topping

100g (4oz) vegan margarine
● 200g (7oz) icing sugar
● 1-2 tablespoons hot water
● 1oz (25g) cocoa

Method

Grease two 8-inch (200mm) sandwich tins and line with greaseproof paper. Heat oven to 170°c/325°f/gas 3.

Sift the flour, cocoa and baking powder into a bowl. Add the sugar,

"Any in the cake?" "Oh plenty sir"

vanilla extract, oil, water and ganja then mix well to a batter-like consistency.

Pour into tins and bake for 35-40 mins. When the cakes are firm to the touch remove from the oven, leave to cool, then turn out onto a wire rack.

For the filling and topping, cream together the margarine and sugar with a little hot water and the cocoa, spread over the cake.

If you have a spare leaf, place it on the cake and sift over with icing sugar until the cake is covered. Carefully remove the leaf for an impressive effect.

Ann's truffles

Named after my dear friend who gave me this recipe, "Now keep it to yourself, or they will all be making them." As a teenager it was my first collected cannabis recipe. So keep it to yourself as she would still kill me if she knew I told you…

Makes 16-20 truffles

Eat 1-2 each

You will need

100g (4oz) chocolate or carob
● 25g (1oz) butter or vegan margarine ● 14g (½ oz) ground leaves 7g (¼ oz) or 3-4 g (⅛ oz) hash or good buds 2g (¹⁄₁₆ oz)
● a double shot of rum or your favourite tipple, Southern Comfort is nice ● 100g (4oz) icing sugar ● 25g (1oz) cocoa or vermicelli or carob again

Method

Melt the chocolate slowly in a bowl over a saucepan which is a quarter-full of water or use a melting pan if you have one. In a separate saucepan, melt the butter and add the ground ganja or crumbled hash (or melt down your ready-made cannabutter, see page 21). Add the rum and stir in.

A busy Ann!

Next add the melted chocolate, stir in well and remove from the heat. Sift in the icing sugar and combine with a spoon until the mixture falls away from the sides of your pan.

Dust your hands with cocoa and roll the mixture into balls, which should be soft and oily. Roll in some cocoa or vermicelli, place on grease-proof paper and pop in the fridge for a while, if you can wait that long.

Mellow marsh mellow

Makes 12-14 mellows

Eat 1-2 each

You will need

100g (4oz) butter ● 3-4 g ($^1/_8$ oz) finely ground light hash 2g ($^1/_{16}$ oz) ● 100g (4oz) white marshmallows ● 100g (4oz) slab of vanilla toffee, chopped up ● 150g (6oz) rice crispies ● 100g (4oz) chocolate

Method

Gently melt the butter, add the powdered hash. Stir occasionally for about 5 minutes at a very gentle simmer.

Then add the mallows and toffee. Once it has all melted add the crispies. Mix in well and remove from the heat. Do not let it boil as you don't want the hash getting too hot.

Spread the mixture onto a greased baking tray. Then melt the chocolate (see recipe opposite) and smear it all over the top. Once it has gone cold it is ready to cut into 12-14 bite-size squares.

English garden

Cous cous, you can...

Serves about 6

You will need

1 courgette ● 1 onion ● 2 peppers red, yellow, or green ● 6-8 baby corns ● 50g (2oz) of feta cheese ● 4 mushrooms ● some olive oil ● 1 pack of easy-to-make cous cous ● knob of butter ● 7g (¹/₄ oz) or for a mellower effect use 3g (¹/₈ oz) good buds chopped finely with scissors over a saucepan to catch all its crystals. Mix with some fresh coriander if you have it. You can of course improvise with all sorts of different mixtures of vegetables.

Method

Heat oven to 220˚c/425˚f/Gas 7.

Chop up the vegetables into large chunky bits, and drizzle over with oil and roast for 30 minutes on the top shelf.

Starting with your saucepan of weed, stir in the cous cous and a knob of butter, put on a gentle heat, then add 1 tablespoon of olive oil and mix in 7fl oz of boiling water.

Take off the heat, and let it sit with the lid on for 5 minutes.

Uncover and cook very gently for a further 2 minutes giving it a regular stir. Then place into an oven proof dish and level out and cover with the roasted vegetables. Switch the oven off, sprinkle the chopped cheese over the vegetables and pop back into the oven for 5 minutes. Serve with some nice crusty bread.

...especially with good guidance

Before...

After

Biryani

Originating from central Asia, biryani is mild, very aromatic and rich in flavour. Made with saffron rice, cooked either with lamb, chicken, fish or vegetables, in a spiced ghee with almonds and sultanas, this is an ideal dish as it is served in small quantities and the spices work very well with the cannabis. Biryani is traditionally served with flat breads and curry dishes.

Serves 6-8

You will need

6 tablespoons of ghee or good oil ● a stick of cinnamon ● 5 cardamom seeds, broken, open to use ● 5 cloves ● 2 cloves of crushed garlic ● 1 teaspoon of chopped ginger ● 1 teaspoon of fennel seeds ● ½ teaspoon chilli powder ● 1kg (2lb) cubed lamb or chicken and or a mix of chopped vegetables ● 300g (5oz) natural yogurt ● 150ml (¼ pint) water ● ½ teaspoon salt ● 500g (1lb) washed and soaked basmati rice ● 2 tablespoons cannabutter or sacred ghee (see pages 21 and 22) ● ½ teaspoon of saffron threads (soaked in 2 tablespoons of boiling water)

For the garnish

2 tablespoons of ghee or oil
● 4 tablespoons flaked almonds
● 4 tablespoons sultanas

Repeat the layers to finish with rice

Method

Heat the oven to 190°c/375°f/ gas 5. Gently heat the ghee or oil in a large pan. Add the cinnamon, cardamom and cloves; within a minute or so you will smell a strong aroma. Now add the garlic, ginger, fennel and chilli powder. Cook for 5 minutes stirring constantly.

Add the meat or vegetables and fry well on all sides. Stir in the yogurt a spoonful at a time followed by the water and a sprinkle of salt; cover and allow to simmer for around 40 minutes.

Fill another large pan two thirds with water bring it to the boil, rinse the rice again and add with the salt to boil for three minutes, then drain.

Now using the 2 tablespoons of sacred ghee or cannabutter, place this evenly around a casserole dish, then cover the bottom with rice and sprinkle with the half of the saffron and its water, then cover with a layer of lamb or vegetables and its liquid. Repeat the layers to finish with rice, cover and cook in the oven for about 45 minutes.

Just before the dish is ready heat a little ghee or oil in a frying pan and sauté the almonds and sultanas gently until they are just turning brown serve sprinkled on top of the biryani.

Biryani is delicious garnished with sultanas and almonds

Carrot and cannabis halva

Makes 8-10 portions

Eat 1 each

You will need

600ml (1 pint) milk ● 100g (4oz) cooked carrots, lightly mashed ● 40g (1 $\frac{1}{2}$ oz) butter ● $\frac{1}{2}$ tablespoon golden syrup ● 50g (2oz) sugar ● 25g (1oz) sultanas ● teaspoon of cardamom ● 3-4g ($\frac{1}{8}$ oz) finely ground good quality hashish 1-2g ($\frac{1}{16}$ oz)

Method

Place milk and carrots in a heavy-based saucepan. Cook on a high heat stirring now and again, keeping close to the boil until all the liquid has evaporated. Add the butter, syrup sugar, fruit and cardamom; lastly add the hashish. Carry on cooking on a lower heat for about 10 minutes, stirring regularly, until the mix starts to come away from the pan. As the mixture is cooling pour evenly into a buttered dish. Allow to set then cut into 8-10 pieces.

Freshly cooked carrots

Freshly made pollen

Pecan pot pie

Makes 6-8 portions

You will need

200g (8oz) pecan or walnuts
● 4 eggs ● 250 ml (9fl oz)
maple syrup ● 2 tablespoon
lemon juice ● ¹/₂ teaspoon
cinnamon ● 1 ¹/₂ teaspoons
vanilla extract ● ¹/₄ teaspoon salt
● 200g (8oz) ready roll short
crust pastry ● 3-4g (¹/₈ oz)
powdered hash not weed
2g (¹/₁₆ oz)

Method

Heat the oven to 180°c/350°f/
gas 4.

Line an 8-inch (200mm) pie dish
with pastry and sprinkle the base
with nuts.

Now beat the remaining
ingredients together and pour into
the pie dish. Bake in the middle
of the oven for 30 minutes.
Remove and allow to cool for
another 30 minutes, before
serving warm with cream.

Gather your ingredients

Spicy bread pudding

Serves 4-6

Save some for me!

You will need

200g (8oz) stale bread ● ¹/₂ pint of milk ● 3-4g (¹/₈ oz) ground hash, a nice fresh pollen gives a wonderful flavour to this great pud 2g (¹/₁₆ oz) ● 100g (4oz) butter ● 75g (3oz) brown sugar ● 50g (2oz) of currants or sultanas ● 50g (2oz) of cherries or dried cranberries ● 1 egg ● 1 level teaspoon ground mixed spice

Method

Remove any hard crusts and break the bread into pieces. Leave to soak in the milk for about an hour. Prepare your hash and combine with the mixed spice.

Place the butter in a small pan and gently melt. Heat the oven to 180°c/350°f/gas 4. Lightly butter a 2-pint (200mm) ovenproof dish.

Squeeze out the excess milk from the bread and break up the lumps into a large bowl with a spoon. Add all the remaining ingredients including the butter and mixed spices to the bowl and blend together well. Add a little milk to keep it loose, drop out into the dish and spread it out evenly. Bake for 1 hour then remove and sprinkle with sugar while it is hot. This is nice served warm with cream.

Weed muffins

Makes 12 muffins

Eat 1-2 each

You will need

225g (8oz) self-raising flour
● pinch of salt ● 1¹⁄₂ teaspoons
baking powder ● 150g (6oz)
grated cheese of your choice
● 3-4g (¹⁄₈ oz) well ground buds
2g (¹⁄₁₆ oz) ● or 7g (¹⁄₄ oz) ground
leaves 3g (¹⁄₈ oz) ● 1 tablespoon
fresh thyme ● 190g (7oz) butter
● 1 egg white, whisked ● 1 egg
yolk ● 260ml milk

Method

Warm the oven to 220°c/425°f
/gas 7. Using a 12-hole muffin
tin, line each one with a paper
muffin case.

Stir together flour, salt and
baking powder in a bowl, then stir

Ready for tea

in the cheese, weed, and thyme.
Put this to one side.

In a pan melt the butter then pour
into a clean bowl. To this add the
whisked egg and yolk with the milk.
Mix together well then stir gently
into the cheese and weed mix.

Spoon enough into each case to
fill and bake for 20-25 minutes
until they are well risen and firm.
Serve one each warm and dripping
with butter.

The winter's air is cold and frosty with the harvest of those fully laden plants now over. The kitchen air is a thick shade of pink, faded from the deep purple haze created from millions of flying crystals. After a good thrashing, the plant matter is then sieved either in the traditional way with large knotted carpets, or with modern day screens. They both do the same important job of collecting all the sticky resin glands.

The first sift gives the best quality, it then becomes weaker with each further sift.

This treasured pile of golden powder is then pressed, usually with a mechanical device, good quality oily cannabis will bind easily this way. However, if it is old and stale, it will need some warming to encourage it to bind. Sometimes the sugary inside pulp of figs is added to the resin, as is fat or condensed milk which acts as a sticky binding agent. At least these are more favourable than candle wax or animal dung!

Plants were made into cannabis resin for the ease of transportation and for its concentrated strength.

However, the oldest method of making cannabis is the hand-rubbed method (you do need a full field of the stuff though). A simple collection of the resin glands is made by walking through the plants twice a day during each season, and gently brushing them with your hands. Using the body's heat, combined with the simple movement of kneading, you can produce the finest sought after hashish shaped into slender finger rolls or flat, round patties. These are a real treat to keep your spirits high through the long winter evenings.

Herb stuffing

Local bird gets a stuffing!

You will need

100g (4oz) chopped bacon

● 6 tablespoon shredded suet

● 200g (8oz) breadcrumbs

● 2 tablespoon chopped parsley

● 2 tablespoon fresh chopped
mixed herbs ● grated rind of half
a lemon ● 1 egg beaten ● dash
of milk or you can use some
brandy or whisky ● salt & pepper
● 1-2 tablespoons ground leaves

Tasty

Method

Grill the bacon lightly and
chop up into small pieces.
In a bowl combine the bacon with
all the remaining ingredients using
enough milk or brandy to bind
the mixture together.

Or simply take a packet of your
favourite stuffing mix and add a
1-2 tablespoons of ground up leaf.
Add water as directed with a dash
of spirit, either a whisky or brandy,
whatever you have in the cupboard.
Then shape into balls and cook in
a moderate oven for 10 minutes.

Alternatively stuff the turkey's
neck end with the stuffing.
(Do not stuff main body – place
a quartered lemon in there).
Cover the bird in foil, which can
then be removed for the last $\frac{1}{2}$
an hour to brown off the skin.

Remember that your turkey
should be fresh or fully defrosted
before weighing and cooking.

Once your bird is stuffed, allow
up to 45 mins per kg at
190°c/375°f/gas 5 to cook.

To check that your bird is
fully cooked insert a skewer
into the thickest part of the thigh,
making sure the juices run clear.
Allow your bird to stand for 20
minutes before serving.

Perfect roast potatoes

Live the life!

You will need

6-8 large potatoes

- 8 tablespoons sunflower oil

Method

Peel potatoes and cut into large chunks. Place in a pan of cold water and bring to the boil for 5 minutes. Remove and drain, then cover with a lid and shake vigorously for as long as you can! This will help to give your potatoes a perfect crispness.

Heat clean oil in a roasting tin at 220°c/425°f/gas 7.

Add the potatoes making sure they are rolled over and covered in hot oil. Roast on the top shelf for 35-40 minutes until golden and crispy.

"From small seeds great green plants will grow, and the day will soon come when we shall be free to weed, wine and dine till after midnight! Free to share pickles and pies, and exchange glistening buds before the judge's eyes".

Busy in the kitchen

Ready for dinner

Figgie pudding

So with a little pre-grind, a shot of whisky and a bowl of figs, I came up with this punchy little pud for you all to try. It was shared out with lots of pre-marchers at one of London's "Legalisation of Cannabis" marches. It went down very well, so it is with their recommendation as well as ours that we bring you some figgie pudding!

Take 100g of butter, soft all over, and the same amount of brown sugar, combine together like sweet lovers. Gently add 300g of soft, fine, plain flour and $1/2$ teaspoon of white baking powder, a pinch of salt and two fresh eggs. Gradually mix in with your sugar lovers on their soft bed of flour.

Use 7g of good stinking weed, dried and ground to a dust. With 200g of Figgie's chopped small as a must. Mixed all in together with a generous splash of whiskey and a simple dash of milk. This is all you will need to make your Figgie pudding thrill.

When the mixture is thick and ready to pour, then slowly in she goes to a greased, medium, heatproof bowl. Placed in a pan half full of water. With a gentle heat to warm its bottom right through. Covered tight with a lid or tied with a paper hat, Leave no peek holes for the greedy cat.

Steam for 2-2 $1/2$ hours, keeping your water bubbles in sight, as they will soon burn if left to run dry. Once firm with a spring in the middle, remove from the heat allow the pudding to cool. Then loosen from the sides and with luck… it should come out whole.

Serves between 8 and 10 friends with custard or cream. Soon to feel an ear to eye grin. Gently rolling into that solstice spin… wrapped tight in foil and placed in a tin, this is a secret you can safely keep for a good few weeks!

Soak in warm brandy

Don't let your leaf get too stoned!

Stoned devils on horseback

Eat 1-3 each

You will need

12 rashers of streaky bacon
● 24 chipolatas ● 7g (¹/₄ oz)
ground leaves 3g (¹/₈ oz)

Method

Take the bacon and cut the rashers in half, roll each chipolata sausage in a light sprinkle of finely ground leaves then wrap up in the bacon. Cook at 190°c/375°f/gas 5 for 20 minutes. These are great at parties or for everyone to eat while you finish the turkey.

"Our greatest wish would be to see the freedom of all those currently held in prison on cannabis charges to be allowed to go home".

Riding high

Vegetarian lasagne

A simple dish – yet so tasty. Very good to freeze ready for the unexpected vegetarian weed eater that pops in for dinner.

You will need

1 tablespoon olive oil ● 1 onion or 2 shallots chopped ● 1 garlic clove crushed ● 500g (1lb) minced Quorn or TVP veggie mince ● 2 mushrooms thinly sliced ● 2 tins of tomatoes or slice 4 medium sized fresh ones ● 1 tablespoon of mixed dried herbs ● 6-8 lasagne sheets or use spaghetti by first placing it in a pan of boiling water until it softens, then use as you would the lasagne sheets

For the sauce

25g (1oz) butter ● 1-2 tablespoons ground weed leaf 3/4-pint of milk ● 150g (5oz) a strong cheese, grated ● 40g (1 1/4 oz) plain flour

Method

Put the oven on to 180°c/350°f/ gas 4. Heat the oil in a large pan; add the onion and garlic and cook the mince for a few minutes, then add the mushrooms and tomatoes. Add herbs and season, then let gently simmer for about 15 minutes.

Making the sauce

Warm the butter in a pan until it has melted, add the flour and ground weed. Stir it in well. Remove from the heat and slowly blend in a little of the milk; then place back on the heat and gradually stir in the remaining milk, whisking lightly to remove any lumps. Bring the sauce to a simmer while stirring and as it begins to thicken, lower the heat and crumble in the grated cheese. Keep stirring for about a minute then turn off heat and season.

Making the lasagne

Complete the dish for cooking by pouring half the mince into a 2-pint (200mm) dish, cover with the lasagne sheets and pour over half the sauce; repeat this process and sprinkle some grated cheese on the top and cook for 45 minutes.

Solstice

A pot of hot pot

You will need

2 parsnips ● 3 carrots
● 2 sticks of celery ● 1 leek
● 50g (2oz) butter ● 2 chopped
onions ● 1 clove of garlic crushed
25g (1oz) flour ● 1 pint of stock
● ¼-pint white wine ● a tin of
washed baked beans ● 200g
(7oz) button mushrooms
● 1 teaspoon mixed herbs
● salt & pepper

Method

Peel and chop the vegetables first,
set the oven to 180°c/350°f/gas 4.

Melt the butter in a large pan,
add the onions and garlic cook
until soft. Stir in the flour and
cook for a few minutes, then
remove from the heat and add
the stock and wine, followed
by all the other prepared
ingredients. Put into a casserole
dish cover with a lid and cook for
an hour.

I know you think I have forgotten
to add the pot to this one! But I
didn't want it to be lost in such a
big dish, you will find it is a lot
better floating on top.

Doped-up dumplings

Serves 5-6

You will need

100g (4oz) self-raising flour
● 25g (1oz) butter ● 50g (2oz)
grated cheese ● 1 teaspoon
mustard powder ● 2-3g (⅛ oz)
ground weed

Method

Place the flour, mustard powder
and weed into a bowl rub in the
butter and stir in the cheese.
Add a little water to make a soft
not sticky dough and divide up in
to 10 balls. Drop these in the pot
after the first hour and remove the
lid and let it all cook for a further
30 minutes.

Uncooked

Ready to eat

Camembert

You will need

A medium size camembert cheese ● 1 onion ● 1 pepper ● 1-2g of good finely ground buds

Method

This is a flavoursome recipe for real cheese lovers. Use a medium size camembert, remove it from its box. Slice the cheese horizontally ¼-inch (6mm) from the top. Put the lid of cheese along with the box to one side.

Finely dice the onion and the pepper and add to the finely ground buds. Evenly spread the mixture into the cheese. Replace the top and gently squeeze it together, so it will fit back in the box.

Place onto a low shelf in a warm oven set at around 150°c/300°f/gas 2.

Before

After

If you begin cooking this at the start of a meal, it will be ready for the cheese and biscuits at the end. Alternatively, you can make some thin slices of toast for cheese dipping when you need a snack.

Mulling-it-over-wine

Cannabis is often added to alcohol to make a quick and effective drink that will keep. This red-hot little number is best drunk on the night of making however, and merriment is sure to follow!

Passing thoughts

Serves 6-8

You will need

1 bottle of good red wine

● **4 cloves** ● ¼ **teaspoon of nutmeg** ● ¼ **teaspoon of cardamom** ● **a stick (or ground) cinnamon** ● **an orange to stick the cloves into** ● **use up your trimmed leaves – around 25g (1oz)** 14g (½ oz)

Method

Place all ingredients into a pan and warm gently for 2 hours. Just strain and serve.

Solstice cake

You will need

200ml (7oz) Madeira or sherry or any good fruity booze ● 25g (1oz) ground leaves 14g ($\frac{1}{2}$ oz) buds and 7g ($\frac{1}{4}$ oz) hashish ● 50g (2oz) apricots (chopped, washed) ● 170g (6oz) glace cherries ● 100g (4oz) mixed peel (washed) ● 50g (2oz) crystallised ginger (chopped washed) ● 50g (2oz) ground almonds ● 50g (2oz) glace pineapple ● 50g (2oz) dried fruit, either pear, papaya or sultanas ● 12oz (340g) plain flour ● 250g (9oz) butter ● 2 teaspoons baking powder ● 250g (9 oz) caster sugar ● 4 eggs (beaten) ● 450g (1lb) jar of apricot jam ● grated rind of a lemon ● 85g (3oz) your choice of mixed fruit and nuts for decoration

NB: Don't forget to halve all these cannabis amounts for therapeutic use.

Tempting!

Method

Pre–heat the oven in mid-November! Seriously though, for the best flavour, this cake should be made up to six weeks before it's eaten. But in an emergency it can be made just a few days before the Solstice. This is one of our strongest recipes and the most loved by visitors. It will get a good 20 people totally smashed.

First place half the sherry or Madeira (85g/3oz) into a pan to warm through. Crumble in the fine hash, stir well and keep on a low heat for about 15 minutes.

Then pour the mixture over the washed and chopped fruit and leave overnight if possible or for a few hours at least.

When you are ready to start cooking, prepare some cannabutter (see page 21) using 150g (3oz) of the butter with all of the grass buds and leaves.

Grease an 8-inch (200mm) cake tin and line with greaseproof paper. Pre-heat the oven to 170°c/325°f /gas 3.

Sift the flour and baking powder into a bowl and set aside. Now add to the bowl of soaked fruit mixture;

Stirring in crumbled hashish

ground almonds, lemon rind and a few spoons of the flour to mix in.

In another bowl, cream together the cannabutter and the remaining butter with the sugar until it is all light and fluffy. Add the beaten eggs, alternating with heaped tablespoons of flour after each egg. Then, stirring well, add the remaining flour.

Next, add to this the fruit mixture and another 100ml (3½ fl oz) of the booze, so the mixture is just pourable.

First, make your wish!

Then turn into the tin and bake for 1½ hours. Then, turn the oven down to 150°c/300°f/gas 2 and continue to bake for a further 1½-2 hours.

Test the cake with a clean skewer by gently inserting it into the centre of the cake, if it appears clean then remove the cake and allow to cool for 10 minutes before turning out onto a wire rack. When the cake is cold, make some small holes in the top and bottom and pour a little of the remaining Madeira or sherry over the cake regularly (about once a week).

Well dissolved

The days are getting longer

This cake will keep for up to 6 weeks if wrapped in foil and kept in a tin. It stays moist and becomes very potent if this is done, so it's well worth the effort.

To decorate your cake, wait until it is about to be eaten. Heat the jam slowly and spread a thin layer over the whole cake. Then cover with a pattern of fruit, nuts and leaves of your choice. Or as I have done sometimes, use a cannabis leaf as a stencil and simply dust over it with icing sugar. Makes a great impression.

Make sure your guests have somewhere to crash out as they don't seem go very far after this.

Adding ground weed to butter

Stirring the fruit

You can only have one wish though!

Coffee anyone?

As in Turkish coffee houses, or in the bars of 16th century Amsterdam, this preparation has been enjoyed for hundreds of years. Here, sailors would trade and drink rich, dark coffee under the dim lights, its sophisticated taste hiding its dark nature. Try our Café Cannabis!

You will need

300ml (½ pint) hot fresh coffee

- ½ teaspoon caster sugar
- 1-2g finely ground hashish
- 1 tablespoon of Tia Maria

(or your favourite liqueur)

Method

Make up some hot fresh coffee in a jug or cafetiere.

Pour into two glass cups and stir into each the caster sugar, hashish and the liqueur.

Then spoon or squirt on some whipped cream and dust in Cocoa.

"Weed is the food of the mind"

Loaded toffee caramels

You will need

85g (3oz) butter ● ¼ can condensed milk (4 tablespoons)

● 225g (8oz) sugar

● 8 tablespoon golden syrup

● ½ teaspoon vanilla essence

100g (4oz) plain chocolate broken up ● 3-4 g (⅛ oz) use a good Moroccan hash finely crumbled or 2g (¹⁄₁₆ oz) (Grass does not work very well in this recipe). You will need a heavy-based pan as this mixture gets extremely hot.

Method

Put everything except the chocolate and hash into a heavy-based saucepan. Stir over a low heat until the sugar has dissolved.

Add the broken chocolate and warm steadily to 120°c. If you don't have a thermometer, put a drop of cold water into a saucer and drop a little of the toffee onto it. As it cools it will show the setting stage that it has reached. For a soft caramel, roll into a soft ball. The hotter it becomes the harder and more toffee like it will be.

Remove the pan from the heat and place on a cold surface. When it has settled and cooled to 60°c, the hash can be gently and safely stirred into the mixture.

After it has cooled down enough to handle, pour into a buttered 8-inch tin. Cut into about 30 squares or roll into éclairs. If you wish to add a touch of luxury dip, the caramels into melted chocolate. These will keep for several weeks wrapped in waxed paper and placed in a tin.

Make your toffees...

...to fill a plate

All burnt out!

Shooting into spring. This is where the fun begins. Planting those tiny seeds to grow into the most laden plants of weed. The sun begins to warm the ground, it stretches ready to be turned. Fresh is the morning air with only a nip left of the cold winter's glare.

To grow this plant should be my right. That right has become my life. So I shall dance on the moon tonight with the crafty old Witch of Weed.

Treading gently as she walks over each new seed bringing life into every tiny golden bead. It's a small and simple start that will eventually warm many a heart, and I can see we are going to need quite a lot of that weed as the café is packed and the ovens are hot! Let's feed this hungry lot.

Eric's sex and grow guide

Cannabis plants are either male, female or hermaphrodite (though this is not common). Female plants are the best plants to grow for consumption as they produce big clumps of flowers covered in resin (and full of THC). Male plants produce small green balls which develop into pollen flowers. These are nice to use in cooking, and although not so strong in THC they are still very enjoyable. If the male is introduced to the female, her flowers will produce seeds rather than buds. So, remember, never grow male and female plants anywhere near each other or you could end up with bags of seed and nothing much to smoke or cook with!

Once your plants start to flower the females will produce small white hair-like pistils at the base of each branch join. Un-pollinated the female will produce fine buds without seeds, this is known as Sensimelia.

Indoor plants will take 6-7 weeks with 24 hours of continuous light before they produce pre-flowers. Outside plants will take a little longer. The males soon give themselves away as they are tall, thin and often straggly looking compared to the girls.

Swings and roundabouts

All from a seed...

A little stick of weed

Male

Female

Indoors or out?

There are pros and cons to both environments here. Indoors it is easier to conceal your plants from prying eyes, and you can create a controlled environment (the perfect world for your cannabis). If you have a greenhouse then you get the best of both worlds. Whereas the benefit of outdoor growing is that the sun and the immense light it produces are absolutely free!

It is hard to reproduce the sun's power indoors, to attempt this you will have to use some high intensity discharge (H.I.D) lamps which can be purchased from any good grow shop. The lamps come in two types, sodium and metal

Back garden

halide. The sodium lamps are used for flowering and metal halides for growing. These lamps produce a lot of heat as well as light which will cause the room to get too hot, so you will need to use extractor fans to reduce the temperature. You will need to achieve a steady temperature of around 75°f-85°f when the lights are on, which will then allow the room to cool down when they are switched off. Being indoors means you can control the cycles by timers and can give the plants 24 hours light through the growing stages, although I feel they do benefit from having some rest time. Once flowering the best cycle is twelve hours continuous light and 12 hours of darkness.

For the outdoor grower this is all taken care of and your cannabis will grow happily when it receives a good 16 hours of uninterrupted daylight followed by 8 hours of continuous darkness. Cannabis plants love the sun, without enough of it they remain thin and weedy and without big-stocked buds.

My place or yours?

Seeds can be obtained for growing both indoors and out. The choice of seed type will depend on where you live and intend planting it to flower. Cannabis indica, originally from central Asia, is probably the most popular plant used in cooler climates. This strain is often crossed with cannabis sativa from the hot climes of India which prefers a more intense heat.

Not as common is the cannabis ruderalis, a wild strain which came originally from Russia. This is a very strong and hardy plant, the cross breeding of these three strains are what produces many of the well known trademark plants that grow as well inside as outside. The selection of seeds available is amazing and you will find *Weed World*, the UK's leading magazine, is a good place to start to find a reputable supplier.

Bring on good seed stock by filling some small pots with seed/cutting compost, then pop a seed into each pot and sprinkle with a little compost. Then moisten the compost with a spray mister and cover with clingfilm. Place on a windowsill or under a low power fluorescent light.

Once they come up (usually within a week or so), remove the clingfilm. After another week or so they will need bigger pots; fill these with a well mixed combination of 2 parts compost, 1 part coco fibre and 1 part perlite, you will find all these or similar composts in your local garden centre. Loosen the plants

Potting on

gently out of their pots, place into the new pot with fresh compost, and using your hands, firm around the stem. Gently water and place back under its lamp or in a safe, sunny spot in the garden. Never let the plants dry out, always give them plenty of water as they love it!

Nip it in the bud

Once you have found a strain you like that grows well, then you can take some cuttings from it. This must be done before the plant finishes flowering. Cuttings are taken in the same way as most hardwood cuttings, which is to cut at a 45° angle, 4-5 leaves down from the tip of the stem you wish to cut.

Starting out on your own

Place the cut end into rooting hormone powder or liquid (available from your garden centre) and place it into a pot filled with cutting compost. Moisten the soil and cover the pot with clingfilm. Then put under a cool white fluorescent tube light or onto the windowsill, the plant should root in 10-14 days.

Indoor plants, depending on the cycle should take from 7-14 weeks to mature. You will know when they are ready as all the white hairs change colour to brown, red and orange, and the buds will seem to swell slightly and look well laden. If you have grown the plants outside they will take 4-6 months to reach maturity.

If you are experiencing problems with disease or pests I would recommend you check out some of the excellent grow guides available at Eric's Kitchen, where you will always find someone happy to help with your choice of books covering all these problems and many more.

Home and dry

Cut down the plants at the base of the stem and hang them up in a warm dry room with circulating air, leaving them for 7-10 days until half dry. They give off a potent smell at this stage.

Split the plants into smaller more manageable bits and put all buds into a large airtight container leaving a small opening for air exchange. Regularly stir them around gently until they are completely dry. Trim off all the bigger leaves from each bud and use these for cooking.

If you have grown outdoors you will also have some larger shade leaves. Although not as strong as the tops these leaves are good for cooking. Cooking increases the effects so even large leaves like these can still be effective.

And that's it – finally we are at that all-important stage ready to enjoy it.

His and hers

Underfed

Chocolate fudge pudding

Makes enough for 8

You will need

100g (4oz) butter ● 100g (4oz) caster sugar ● 2 eggs ● 75g (3oz) self-raising flour ● 2 tablespoons cocoa powder ● 1-2 tablespoons milk ● 25g (1oz) chocolate chips ● cream to serve ● 4g (¹/₈ oz) ground buds of sparkling weed 2g (¹/₁₆ oz)

To make the sauce

2 tablespoons cocoa powder ● 100g (4oz) soft brown sugar ● ¹/₂-pint boiling water

Caught!

Method

Put the oven on to 190°c/375°f/gas 5. Place all the pudding ingredients into a bowl or processor and mix well then pour into a 2 ¹/₂-pint oven proof dish, and leave to one side.

To make the sauce, place the cocoa and sugar into a bowl and add the hot water mixing well then pour this over your pudding and bake for about 40 minutes. You may wish to try your luck and turn it out whole to reveal the thick sauce below.

To do this allow to cool for five minutes and you will notice the sides shrinking away from the dish. It should come out now, or just spoon out each portion.

Ready to serve warm with a thick double cream.

Fairy cakes or the witches mistake

Anyone who has tried making a plain sponge with weed in will have found that it turns the whole thing green! This might look good for a broccoli bake a green sponge looks very odd!

So we recommend that cocoa or coffee are added to hide the colour and to give your sponge a nicer flavour. Divide the sponge up into individual cases for easy portions. This mix makes about 24 individual cakes, but don't eat too many at once!

You will need

150g (5oz) plain flour ● 170g (6oz) margarine ● 170g (6oz) sugar • 25g (1oz) cocoa ● 25g (1oz) grated chocolate ● 3 eggs ● 3 teaspoon baking powder ● a drop of milk or teaspoon of made up coffee ● 3-4g (1/8 oz) hash or good buds 1-2g (1/16 oz) or 14g (1/2 oz) leaves 7g (1/4 oz)

For the icing

200g (7oz) icing sugar ● 1-2 tablespoons of hot water

Method

Warm the oven to 180°c/350°f/ gas 4. Put everything into a food processor and switch on for two minutes, or put it all into a bowl and beat like mad! Then pour into two

Fun and cake games

greased sponge tins or fill lots of little paper cake cases with a generous teaspoon in each and bake for 15-20 minutes. Then remove and allow to cool on a wire rack.

Sponges can be tested for readiness by pressing the top, it should spring back and be golden. Spike it with a skewer to make sure – if it comes out clean it's ready.

To make the icing, beat the ingredients in a bowl until the mixture is light and creamy.

Eric's cannabis cookies

These days its easy to cheat and buy a cookie mix and add your prepared cannabis then cook as instructed. However, these recipes are so simple you could just as easily make your own, this mix makes between 40-45 delicious cookies. This is one of the house favourites!

You will need

100g (4oz) butter ● 100g (4oz) white sugar ● 85g (3oz) soft brown sugar ● ½ teaspoon vanilla essence ● 7g (¼ oz) finely powdered hashish 3-4g (⅛ oz) ● 1 egg ● 230g (8oz) self raising flour ● ½ teaspoon salt ● 100g (4oz) chocolate chips ● 50g (2oz) chopped walnuts or nuts of your choice

Method

Warm the oven to 190°c/375°f/gas 5.

Cream together butter, sugar, and vanilla essence with prepared hashish. Add a lightly beaten egg followed by the flour and salt beat well.

Then add the chocolate chips and chopped nuts. Shape the mixture into teaspoon-sized balls and place in lines onto lightly greased baking trays, leaving some space between them so they can spread out a little. Bake for 10-15 minutes until golden brown and the whole of your kitchen smells edible.

Allow them to cool before tucking in. Be warned that these are so easy to eat that I always make an extra batch without any cannabis in ready for the munchies, and for the kids, as they seem to have a built in radar that tells them chocolate chip cookies are being made!

Food for the eye

This is such a fascinating area of cannabis use that these few pages can only just touch on this vast subject based on the basic instinct that you know when something is good for you. Once discovered as a medicine, its use has continued for thousands of years as millions of qualified and unqualified persons like myself have self administered cannabis and felt its remarkable yet gentle effects with its versatility to help cope and heal many an ailment or mood. Having witnessed the relaxing and untwisting of rheumatic hands and seen the joy of sight restored to a bewildered and stoned recipient, used to the constant haze of Glaucoma. Helping after chemotherapy for cancer easing the nausea in those difficult early days of recovery. As a gentle pain relief that can make a day of illness far more bearable. Calming the muscle spasms of Multiple Sclerosis offering some help to others living with Epilepsy, Arthritis, Migraine and Aids as it stimulates the appetite as well as other things! Recorded for its analgesic, antibiotic, and anti-inflammatory properties, it soon takes effect to calm both the body and mind by relaxing tense muscles and widening your thoughts away from the pain.

At home...

...with Clare Hodges who has long campaigned for the right to use cannabis as a symptom-reducing drug for Multiple Sclerosis. Sadly it is not going to go away, but is controlled with the use of cannabis, effectively helping her to cope with a disease which affects not only the eyesight and speech, but the body too. This will become weaker with the onset of a tingling sensation which in time progresses, often in the hands and arms,

Eric invites Clare Hodges to check out the merchandise...

eventually sending the muscles into spasm and tremors, making life very difficult.

This weakness also affects the functions of the bowel and bladder, and a general loss of balance means extra difficulties in walking often leaving no choice but for the person to reluctantly become wheelchair bound.

Those brave souls who have had to defy the law so they can take some relief from this terrible debilitating disease have no other choice as Clare knows so well. Whilst not all patients want to smoke, some find a little cake or chocolate is the best way to fight back. Not all wanting to be high from the effects, simply lowering the cannabis can help to find a suitable balance although each batch will differ depending on the quality of cannabis used.

Cannabis is uncommonly good at being used alongside other prescribed medication, all working to give an improvement and some life back. The evidence was obvious on the day when Clare admitted she had not cooked for a long time, she smoked a neat joint, and was able to get up and help prepare one of Eric's simple snacks for lunch. What a treat to chat and see her lovely smile light up!

Tempting toast

And this is what we did...

You will need

a few slices of wholemeal bread
● 100g (4oz) tasty Dutch Gouda
(or use a strong cheddar cheese)
● 1 tablespoon milk ● a small
knob of butter ● 1-2 teaspoon of
ground weed ● ½ teaspoon of
wholegrain mustard ● 1-2
tomato's ● 2 slices of ham

Method

Take a slice of wholemeal bread for
each person. Toast one side while
you grate the cheese.

Then, in a small pan gently melt
the cheese with the milk, the
butter, and add the ground weed
and mustard with a little grind of
black pepper.

Then on the un-toasted side of
the bread spoon on some of the
cheese mixture and layer it with
a few slices of tomato and some
thin sliced ham. Then pour over
the remaining cheese and weed
mixture, and grill it under a
medium heat until it is lightly
toasted and ready to eat.

Can I eat this now?

Herb and bacon pie

Serves 5-6

You will need

225g (8oz) pre-pack puff or short crust pastry ● 250g (½lb) sliced lean rashers of bacon ● 2 small leeks, washed and chopped ● 1-2 tablespoon of fresh buds finely chopped ● 1 tablespoon of your favourite fresh herbs (parsley, thyme, and savoury) finely chopped ● 4fl oz single cream or milk ● 2 eggs ● salt and pepper

Chef shows us how it's done

Method

Heat oven to 190°c/375°f/gas 5. Grease and line a pie dish or a dozen small ones with the pastry and trim the edges with a knife. You can pre-bake the pastry so that the base is firmer (known as baking blind). Cover in greaseproof paper and scatter with some dried pulses or beans to weigh it down while it cooks for 10 minutes in the middle of the oven. Then remove and discard paper and pulses.

Fry the bacon in its own fat until cooked. Chop into small pieces and sprinkle half over pastry then cover with the leek and all the weed and herbs and then sprinkle over the remaining bacon.

Whisk together cream or milk with eggs, salt and pepper. Pour over each pastry evenly ready to bake on the top shelf for 30-35 minutes until the filling has set.

Serve with a green salad.

A helping hand

Eating cannabis requires half an hour or so longer to take effect than smoking as it has to be absorbed into the kidneys first. This changes the way you react and it creates a more intense legless feeling, that can last for about 3-4 hours.

It has a history of being used in childbirth, one use which I personally favoured. And for menstrual cramps, a true god send.

Cannabis is a safe and gentle plant to use, there have been no direct deaths from the over consumption of cannabis. Animals also benefit and it has been widely used in veterinary preparations to make many different tablets, pills, capsules, tinctures, creams and lotions. Like us, animals usually take cannabis with ease. The main danger to a sick person is the risk of using a contaminated product which has seen the use of pesticides or other unknown substances in its production. This situation could be extremely dangerous. So back yard growing has to be the best as it can ensure a clean healthy product. Of course, this would also be the case in future licensed cannabis outlets.

For many people cannabis insures a good night's sleep, leaving them feeling fresh and motivated in the morning, unlike a hangover. As the cannabis takes affect most people find themselves relaxing, falling into chatter and laughter until dry and parched, when instinctively they return to the kitchen in need of a drink and something to eat!

Cannabis is not recommended, however, for people or even animals that are depressed, confused or have any form of mental illness as they will find that it is not a benefit to use cannabis as it can cause paranoia and can exaggerate worries and problems, so it is not advised. If you don't like the feeling of being stoned, just sleep it off. It just does not suit some people. Still it's safer than a peanut to most.

Check with your doctor if you are taking other prescribed medicine. Alternatively, check with your drug dealer if the drugs you are taking have not yet been legalised where you live.

Tinctures

You will need

600ml (1-pint) alcohol to every 25g (1oz) of dried buds, or if you are using leaves use 50g (2oz) to every 600ml (1-pint)

Method

Tinctures are easily made using dried grass finely ground and covered in alcohol. This is best done in a dark glass bottle with a screw lid, allowing the tincture to rest for two weeks in a dark warm place before use. Always make sure utensils are sterilised with boiling water.

The alcohol needs to be at least 60 per cent alcohol content or even higher. Vodka is the most readily available. Give the mixture a good shake once a day and then after two weeks strain through a fine filter and store in a dark tinted glass bottle to preserve the tincture. This can now be taken directly or added to drinks or food. Try one drop at first as the potency can vary.

An easy to make drink

You will need

1-2 grams ground fine grass
- a good shot of whisky

Method

Mix the ingredients together in a glass in the morning and leave until the afternoon. Then, add a little boiling water and a dash of lemon juice and create a drink to see you through the evening!

Ointment

You will need

50g (2oz) Vaseline ● 50g (2oz) butter ● 25g (1oz) finely ground leaves

Method

This is also easily made using Vaseline warmed in a pan with butter and finely ground leaves for 10 minutes. Pour back into the Vaseline jar and store in a dark place. This can now be rubbed on aching, tired joints or onto dry rough skin. It is absorbed into the skin with soothing effects, although it does not get you stoned.

Poultices

The large shade leaves can be soaked in alcohol and then wrapped directly onto swollen joints, or they can be pulped and warmed with a little water and placed on the affected area such as sores, ulcers, and sunburn. Hold in place with a wrap of wet cloth.

Hemp leaves are just as useful, as the body does not absorb the THC from topical application.

Hemp oil those body bits

Using some warmed hemp oil rub gently into your hair and cover with a warm towel and leave for about 1 hour (make sure no one is coming round!) makes a great boosting conditioner. This is best used about once a month.

Hemp oil can be rubbed directly onto dry skin. You only need a little, as it is thick and very much like a good olive oil. It goes a long way and is very effective, it can also be added to your favourite 100 per cent natural essential oil and used in a relaxing bath or as a base for a soft massage oil.

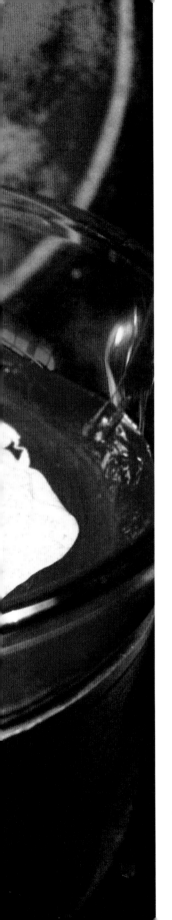

Cocoa beans are picked then set out to dry and ferment in the warm African sun. Inside the bean pods the pulp evaporates and the bean then develops its desirable chocolate flavour. The outer skin is removed and the beans are dried out a little more before being shelled for their precious kernels tucked inside. These are ground and processed into a paste called cocoa solids. It is the proportion of the cocoa solids which determines the quality of a good chocolate product.

This is then pressed to remove some of the cocoa butter, the fat that makes chocolate so good at absorbing all the potency of cannabis. It is then processed further to provide a wide range of textures and flavours, all of which easily blend with cannabis in their own unique way. Mark shows us how its done at the UK's first cannabis chocolate factory.

A chocolate shared...

THC4MS kindly allowed us to join them during a day's chocolate making. In return, they wanted to thank their donors through our pages. As they rely solely on the donations of chocolate and cannabis given to them, so they may distribute it free of charge to the many Multiple Sclerosis sufferers that need it, making the donors essential.

Mark preparing the next batch of cannabis chocolate

...is a friend made

Mark also cares and loves Lesley who sadly has M/S and is the driving force behind the brave work they do as they struggle to keep up with the demand from sick people who can no longer grow a plant or have the strength left to roll a joint, let alone find a dealer. For them they provide an invaluable service all of which is non-profit making. Excusing of course, that last well earned lick of the bowl...

While chocolate melts...

Lesley and Eric discuss the chocolate's excellent possibilities as a hand cream

Chocolate factory

You don't have to climb a mountain if you want to make good chocolate.

The best chocolate will keep in a cool dry place or in the refridgerator for up to one year. You should wrap it well as if you don't it will only keep for about a month, and it might pick up other flavours. Each finished 150g bar has an average of 3g (1/8 oz) of ground weed in it. Generally it is used therapeutically over a seven day period. However, the dosage can differ from one person to another. Using 2 kilos of milk chocolate in the melting machine which has a handy timer so he can even carry on melting chocolate in his sleep, I am impressed! He then places 50g (2oz) of buds and leaves into the electric grinder. In a few minutes it is well ground. Once the chocolate has completely melted, in goes the weed, its sticky crystals clinging to the grinder before being scrapped into the thick gloopy chocolate. You can easily do this at home with a bowl over a pan of simmering water, don't go off to bed though! Stir the weed in well as its potent and peppery smell soon fills the air. Make sure it is thoroughly dispersed, and keep the heat lowered down so as not to burn. Let it gently warm for a few minutes. If you do not have chocolate moulds you can cool it down to about 30°c and then it is possible to pour onto a cold slab and shape by scraping up with spatulas.

You can always return it to the pan if it has cooled too quickly and warm it up to a workable thickness again. Using the moulds involves a process of spooning the chocolate in and then scraping the top to give a smooth base with a few gentle taps to try and remove any air bubbles. If you have trouble removing some air bubbles place the moulds of chocolate onto a washing machine through a spin cycle. This is guaranteed to give you a smooth air-free bar! Then place into the fridge for about two hours to set.

United together...

Milk, white and plain

Melting pot

Plain Chocolate: This can contain anything from 30 to 75 per cent cocoa solids and has a bittersweet flavour. The higher the cocoa content, the richer, smoother and better it will be. Weed gives it a ginger taste, it is the easiest and most popular type used in cooking. ● **Milk Chocolate:** This contains added milk, which makes it creamy and sweeter. It is a little more sensitive to heat and care is needed when using it. However, the final results are just as good as the dark chocolate. Added cannabis hashish gives a slightly honey taste to the chocolate which is very nice. ● **White Chocolate:** This is lower in both cocoa butter and solids. It is the most difficult to cook with as it overheats easily, and turns to a wonderful shade of green with added weed! ● **Cocoa Powder:** This is the powder left behind after all the butter has been pressed from the roasted beans. It is strong and dark, so very good for dusting sweets and flavouring cakes.

Hot chocolate

Love your cooking and it will love you back!

Home on the range

Micro coco

You can make your chocolate in a microwave as well as in a melting pan.

You will need

7g (¼ oz) of some good quality hashish or buds 3-4 g (⅛ oz) ● 150g (6oz) of good milk or dark chocolate ● 1 oz chopped or whole nuts or dried fruit

Method

Prepare your cannabis so it is ready to add as soon as the chocolate has melted.

Break the chocolate into pieces and place into a glass microwave bowl. Put into the microwave oven on full heat for half a minute, then repeat until it's all melted then add crumbled hashish or some very finely ground buds. Stir this in and cook for a further half minute on a medium heat, return to the heat again if necessary making sure the chocolate is well melted.

Now stir in some chopped nuts, such as pecans, brazils, or some dried fruit, or you can keep them whole and dip them into the chocolate (either way you always get in a mess). If you have not got any chocolate moulds you can use the plastic trays from used chocolate boxes. They work well and give you a selection of different shapes to create in. If you make up a nice box for a present make sure it is well labelled and stored out of reach of tiny hands.

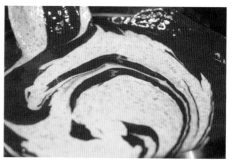

Gently stirred

Enjoy a beautiful chocolate

Set out your ingredients, which should consist of some beautiful glistening buds. Lay them on the table, as if innocent sticks of candy dipped in a fine white sugar, they tempt you. As you breathe in, its power hits you, like the

Poured into moulds

opening of a smelling salts jar. Stoned already, then let's have a look.

The ideal content for medicinal cannabis is for it to contain both THC and CBD at a fifty, fifty mix in the weed. But it is hard for us to measure its content so the trick is to use a mixture of different good crops using both dried leaves and buds. It should easily grind up to a fine dust. You can also use cannabis resin successfully, warming it so that it will easily go into a fine crumble and it can be added just the same.

Ready to eat

Hope you are enjoying your visit to Eric's Kitchen. The air is thick and pungent with a local sweet weed, its buds are beautiful, tight clusters of shiny crystals and little ginger hairs. It would surely win a prize if it could be put on show and admired by others. Freshly made into a golden piece of hash, really soft with a nice flavour, it is so very light and fluffy that it easily crumbles without much help. This is going to make enough for two people to get really smashed if they eat it all to themselves.

Afternoon haze

Serves 2

You will need

1-2g ($^1/_{16}$ oz) hashish ● 75g (3oz) plain or milk chocolate ● 100ml (3$^1/_2$ fl oz) double cream ● 25g (1oz) butter ● 1 tablespoon whisky or your favourite spirit or liqueur

Method

First warm your hashish using a large metal spoon over a gentle low heat. It will soon begin to crumble to a fine powder, which you then set aside. Break the chocolate up into pieces. Using a small pan heat the cream to just boiling then remove from the heat and add the chocolate, butter, booze and hashish. Mix well until the chocolate has melted and is smooth then pour into two small pots or cups and pop into the fridge.

Now for the hardest part, waiting, which gives us enough time to put the kettle on and make a nice cup of cappuccino to go with a spliff. Oh, and then there is all the washing up, of one pan! Now just relax and enjoy, as the rest of the afternoon becomes a... beautiful haze.

In weight this book does not fit the scale!

Sweet moderation

This is a recipe for a whisky and marmalade ice cream, lightly dusted with cannabis crystals and drizzled in a hot orange sauce

Eat 1-2 each

You will need

350g (12oz) good quality orange and whisky marmalade ● 600 ml (20fl oz) whipping cream ● 25g (1oz) caster sugar ● 1 teaspoon orange juice ● 3 teaspoon whiskey

For the saucy sauce!

250g (9oz) orange and whisky marmalade ● 2 tablespoon whisky ● 2 tablespoon orange juice

Method

Take a dusting of a female's fine crystals, or you can use the male's pollen flowers (enough to fill 1-2 dessert spoons).

Place all the ingredients into a processor whizz briefly and pour into an airtight container to chill for an hour then freeze for 1½ hours. Now the mix should be freezing around the edges but still slushy in the middle. Using a hand beater or processor beat well and then return to the freezer for 1½ hours and beat again then freeze for another 4 hours until firm all over. The THC is quite happily frozen and will stay potent for a long time.

To make the sauce, warm the ingredients gently in a pan ready to serve hot and drizzled over the ice cream.

Where are your limits?

Stuffed dates

This is an old and well known North African recipe.

You will need

12 of the best dates

● ½-**1 tablespoon of finely ground hashish** ● **1 tablespoon ground almonds** ● **1 tablespoon ground pistachios** ● **a little honey**

Method

These well-disguised and innocent looking dates are often to be found stuffed with the best hashish. It is quite amazing just how much you can fit into each date!

And if it's not stuffed neat then it can be made into one of these traditional sweetmeats.

Using good dates, first split and remove the stones. Mix equal amounts of good powdered hashish with ground almonds and pistachios. Then stir in a little honey to make a thick green paste ready to place a little into each date.

I laughed and laughed
I laughed so much I cried, great
tears as big as tigers' eyes.
I laughed so much I nearly died.

Microwaving cannabis takes a few seconds...

...the effects of eating it are 2-3 hours of slowly drifting away. When microwaves first moved from the catering trade into our homes people were unsure of using them for heating cannabis. But, used with caution, it is a good form of quick warming to soften hard hashish. The microwave should always be used at a medium setting in 30 second blasts so you don't over cook the cannabis, as it is easy to burn. So don't wander off to watch the television leaving the microwave to smoke your hash!

The microwave can also be used to dry off freshly picked leaves as you can do successfully with other herbs. This does not affect the potency again as long as it is not overcooked.

To do this, lay a paper towel on the turntable, spread the leaves evenly on to the surface. Cover with another paper towel and place in a cup of water. Stick to the 30 second blasts.

You will find the flavour is increased, and they will soon be dry. When cooking, stay within reach of your microwave at all times! If recipes contain a lot of sugar they should be done in a glass bowl as plastic tends to melt. The cooking times vary from one machine to another so check regularly and remember when you take things out they continue to cook for a further minute or so.

Use shade leaves for the first few attempts until you are confident of the exact cooking times, which once found will always remain the same. I have found small dishes are safer to use without burning.

Butter can be easily warmed on a medium setting for 1 minute or if you heat for a further 2-3 minutes, you can remove the skim from the top to give you a clarified butter ready to make the sacred ghee on page 22.

Sensemilla sparkle

Ganjah candy

In 1860, the Ganjah Wallah Hashish Co. USA made and sold Maple Sugar Candy with added hashish that was very popular. Why not try our simple microwave recipe?

1 or 2 will pass the time!

You will need

(50g) 2oz butter ● (350g) 12oz soft brown sugar ● (150ml) ¼-pint milk ● ½ teaspoon vanilla essence ● prepared cannabis 3-4g (⅛ oz) hashish 1-2g (¹/₁₆ oz) (This recipe is better made with cannabis resin)

Method

Place butter in a deep glass dish and melt for 2 minutes. Add all the ingredients apart from the hash. Cook uncovered for 3-4 minutes until it begins to boil. Remove from the microwave oven and stir well.

Return and cook for a further 4 minutes, remove and stir. Cook again for a further 4 minutes, remove from the heat and allow the mixture to settle and cool slightly, then stir in your finely prepared hashish and beat until it gleams. Pour into an 8 inch (200mm) buttered tin. When it sets, break into bite size pieces.

Sweet sticky candy

Pizza the action

Buy a ready made pizza with your favourite toppings. Then simply add a sprinkle of herbs including some weed, cover with cheese and cook, in a moderate oven, for 10 minutes.

If you're in the mood to knock up a base and make up some of your own toppings be sure to include plenty of cheese to get the best from those added herbs! Or call in the party chefs to get things started!

Check this out for a 12-inch base!

You will need

450g (1lb) plain flour ● 1 sachet instant dried yeast ● ½ teaspoon salt ● 175 ml (6fl oz) warm water ● 2 tablespoons oil (hemp oil is great if you have got it)

Method

Place all the ingredients into a bowl gently mixing them together into a dough. Then turn out onto a clean lightly floured surface and give it a good kneed for about 5 minutes.

You wouldn't... would you?

Place into a large bowl, cover loosely with a damp cloth and leave to double its size, then punch it down and press into a well greased 30-cm (12-inch) flan tin (or two smaller ones). Alternatively, place and shape on to a large baking sheet. Leave in a warm place to prove for 15 minutes while you prepare the topping.

Green tree and stilton pizza

You will need

250g (8oz) broccoli ● 50g (2oz)
Stilton ● 100g (4oz) cream
cheese ● 1 tablespoon chopped
chives ● 4-6 cherry tomatoes
● 1-2 tablespoons ground weed

Method

Chop the broccoli up into small
trees, wash and steam for about
5 minutes. Meanwhile blend
together in a bowl the cheeses,
ground weed and herbs.

Spread over the base and top
with the drained broccoli and
some thinly sliced tomatoes.
Place in a hot oven at 220˚c/
425˚f/gas 7. Place on the top
shelf for about 10-15 minutes.

Serve with a fresh garden salad.

Freshly picked

Well mixed

Traditional pizza

Serves 4-6

You will need

100g (4oz) mushrooms, sliced
● 1 onion sliced ● 1 clove garlic,
crushed ● 1 green pepper,
chopped ● 100g (4oz) mozzarella
cheese, sliced ● a few chopped
cherry tomatoes, halved
● a drizzle of olive oil
● 4 tablespoons tomato puree
● a pinch dried savoury and
oregano ● 1-2 tablespoon
ground weed

Method

Roast the mushrooms, onion,
garlic, pepper and tomatoes
in the olive oil in a hot oven
220°c/425°f/gas 7 for
10 minutes.

Cover the base in tomato puree
then top with roasted vegetables
herbs and weed and finally top
with slices of mozzarella cheese.

Bake for about 10-15 minutes
on the top shelf.

Extra toppings by the gram!

Going Dutch for lunch

Serves 2

You will need

225g (8oz) of nice young fresh asparagus ● ½-1 teaspoon ground buds ● butter 25g (1oz) or use cannabutter (page 21) ● 8 slices of fresh bread ● 170g (6oz) Edam or Gouda cheese, thinly sliced ● 110g (4oz) salami sausage or ham (thinly sliced)

Method

Trim the ends of the asparagus and cook them in a little simmering water until tender. Then cream the ground weed and butter together and spread evenly on 4 slices of bread. Then cover with a sprinkle of cheese topped with a slice of salami or ham followed with some stems of the cooked and tender asparagus. Cover each with another slice of bread and place between two grill racks and toast on both sides under the grill.

Freedom

Jacket potatoes

Drenched in cannabutter this is a favourite with most of us. Use on your cooked hot potato(s) along with your favourite topping.

You will need

2-3 baked jacket potatoes ● 25g (1oz) butter ● 1/2-1 teaspoon ground leaf weed ● 1 teaspoon pesto sauce ● some chopped spring onions, peppers, tomatoes

Method

Wash, then cook the potatoes in a hot oven for about an hour or in the microwave for about 10 minutes (however, they are nicer if you can finish them off in a conventional oven).

Take the butter and warm gently add the ground leaf, and simmer very gently for 5 minutes, remove and allow to cool.

Sauté the pesto sauce in a little olive oil with some chopped spring onions, peppers and tomatoes or use a mixture of any of your favourite jacket potato fillings. Then when your potatoes are ready, mash in some of the weedy butter and top with filling.

Chopped...

Topped...

Drenched!

Smoking hot rolls

You will need

50g (2oz) softened butter
● clove of garlic ● ½-1 teaspoon ground buds ● two half-baked bread rolls ● 50g (2oz) sliced smoked pork sausage ● 50g (2oz) blue cheese, crumbled ● 2 tablespoons Greek yoghurt

Method

Warm the oven to 180°c/350°f/gas 4.

Combine together the butter, crushed garlic and ground weed.

Slice two deep cuts through each roll trying not to cut right through, then spread the cuts with the weed and garlic butter. Fill one cut on each roll with the pork sausage and then mix together the crumbled blue cheese and yoghurt to fill the second cut on each roll.

Bake on a baking tray in the middle of the oven for 10-15 minutes. Delicious!

Fancy lunch?

You should always wash seeds thoroughly before grinding them or soaking them in water until they start to sprout. This softens the shell, and gets them ready to add to your recipe. They can be lightly toasted on a baking tray, when the first one pops remove from the heat, ready to add to soups, salads, curries, pasta.

Seeds are delicate and will turn rancid soon after being exposed to cooking. It is advised you eat them within 24 hours of preparation.

They are also pressed and made into a luscious oil, which has a nutty richness to it. It is easily digestible and even suitable for shallow frying if used with an equal amount of olive oil. However, it is not suitable for high heat deep-frying. It should be used as you would a good olive oil.

Hemp oil is also very good when used externally on poor skin. Once open, it will last for the recommended 6 months if kept in the fridge or freezer away from light, in a well sealed brown bottle.

If it is required on a daily basis as a nutritional supplement, then 1-tablespoon is adequate. Choose a good quality, cold pressed oil as it is superior as it does not come into contact with high heat during its production thus helping to protect its nutritional content. Bubble to burst!

Hemp star milk (Houma)

Originating from Ancient China, the following preparation is sacred and an inspiring recipe, which comes from the kind hands of Hempseed Organics.

You will need

a drop of love and some clean hands ● 120g (4oz) organic hemp seed ● 1-pint of distilled or filtered water (warm) ● 7 almonds ● fruit or vegetable juice of your choice

Method

First wash your hands. Then clean through the seeds throwing, out any small green immature or damaged ones. Place into a bowl and cover with water. Stir gently and scoop out all the healthy floating seeds. Place the clean seeds into a bowl with almonds and soak for 8 hours then change the water and continue to soak for a further 36 hours, changing the water regularly to stop any fermentation.

The seeds will start to split and poke out their tails after soaking. They are now ready to drain and grind in your pestle and mortar, adding a drop of water and love. It's hard work by hand. Using a grinder is easier.

Place into a jug and add warm distilled water and stir gently, leaving to rest for 10 minutes. Prepare your fruit or vegetable juice, then strain the milk gently into a clean jug, ready to drink. You can drink it as it is or add your chosen juice, (banana and mango are especially good). The milk sadly has no shelf life and must be drunk straight away.

Cannabis can be added to the hemp star milk when it is finally resting in warm water for the last 10 minutes. The natural fat of the seeds will absorb the THC, recreating this ancient method of preparing a potent drink or cooking juice without the use of any animal fats, sugars or alcohol.

Thanks to the Eden Project (Cornwall)

"Coming out"

Hemp seed milk

Hemp contains just small traces of THC (delta 9 –Tetrahydrocannabinol) so there is no high to be gained from eating the seeds and the same goes for the hemp leaves.

This does not stop them being extremely useful in many other ways as they can be freely used, the seeds for their outstanding nutritional value and the leaves for everything from rope to paper and cloth to food.

The leaves can be ground down to a simple (gluten free) flour and used instead of wheat flour.

Hemp seed contains 500 calories per 100 grams. Soluble fibre makes up 3% of the seed, containing approx. 32% insoluble C60 organic carbon fibre, and 20-25 % protein. Approx. 30% of the seed is unsaturated fat and is the lowest in saturated fats at 8% of total oil volume. This gives us the highest total percentage of Essential Fatty Acids known alongside other common plants. The seeds also contain a whole range of important minerals and vitamins including A, B1, B2, B6, B3, C, D and E.

Bottled seeds

You will need
100g (4oz) clean soaked hemp seeds ● 25g (1oz) almonds ● 1-2 figs to taste

Method
Blend all the ingredients in a food processor with two tablespoons of cold water. Then add a pint of cold water and chill for one hour.

Hemp dressing

The next three recipes were kindly shared with us thanks to Derek from the kitchens of Hemp Union.

You will need

6 tablespoons hemp oil

● **2 tablespoons wine vinegar**

● ½ **teaspoon ground coriander or cumin** ● **2 cloves of garlic**

● **2 lemons** ● **black pepper**

● ½**-1 teaspoon powdered hashish (Eric's little added extra)**

Method

Put all ingredients into a screw top jar "and shake it baby".

If you have them, place a few whole cannabis leaves into the oil. This is guaranteed to get them talking at the dinner table about your dressing, no matter what outfit you have got on.

Trapped

Fruity hemp seed flap jack

Makes 6-8 pieces
Eat one at a time!

You will need

85g (3oz) butter or vegetarian margarine ● 50g (2oz) light brown sugar ● 2 tablespoons golden syrup ● 3-4g ($\frac{1}{8}$ oz) ground weed or powdered hash 2g ($\frac{1}{16}$ oz) or 7g ($\frac{1}{4}$ oz) ground leaves 3-4g ($\frac{1}{8}$ oz) ● 50g (2oz) oats ● 40g (1$\frac{1}{2}$ oz) washed hemp seed ● 85g (3oz) fruit muesli mix

Method

Put the oven on to warm at 180°c/350°f/gas 4. In a large saucepan, melt the butter, sugar and syrup adding your cannabis. Then add in the oats, hemp seed and muesli mixture, mixing well. Then turn onto a greased medium -sized baking tray, pressing well down and out to the edge of the tray. Bake for 15-20 minutes until golden brown, leave to cool for a few minutes then cut into 6-8 pieces.

One in a milliion!

Hemp oil and maple dressing

You will need

3 tablespoons balsamic vinegar

- 6 tablespoons hemp oil
- 1 teaspoon cumin powder
- 3 tablespoons maple syrup
- 1-2 teaspoons of ground

grass or 1/2-1 teaspoon of

crumbled hashish

Method

Put all ingredients into a screw-top jar or bottle and shake well. Store in the fridge, you can experiment with different oils and other herbs such as tarragon and thyme.

For those salad days

Weed and wine

Cannabis and alcohol have always been seen to play out their different social roles, in terms of modern socialising and relaxing at least, on different and sometimes opposing stages. One has only to look at even the most forward thinking and liberal of countries (Holland et al) to see that they are mostly kept very separate. (Although it is permitted for a selected few premises, to allow the consumption of both a fine drop of the old claret and a lovely toke of Nepal's finest).

While the puritanicals in both camps seem set on their images of the happy hippy smoker playing a separate and distinct role from that of the wine-quaffing socialite, we all know, in reality, a truly special evening involves creating a union, perhaps even a holy trinity, of good food, fine wine and some top quality herbal stimulant.

Wine and food are seen as a natural and complimentary partnership. As a result, with the increasing acceptance of the use of cannabis as a unique cooking ingredient, the subject of wine for cannabis food is bound to arise. Before moving forward, however, please note that the effects of cannabis on an inebriated person can be a messy experience. The wine needs to remember it is complimenting an overall experience, when ganja joins it at the table.

Whilst the flavour of cannabis is distinct, it must be assumed we cannot match a single style of wine to all food products made with our favourite hash or weed. The wine will need to marry up to the other ingredients and overall style of the meal or snack depending on the dish's key characteristics. Is the dish sweet? Is it salty? How spicy is the meal? Or how rich is the sauce? In fact, the same decisions we would make when using any other ingredients.

It is easy to say drink what you enjoy. If somebody wants to drink a dry white with roast beef or a big Aussie Shiraz with that grilled salmon then fair enough. However, it is a fact that certain wines suit certain foods. Just as certain foods suit certain types of cannabis.

The first rule is to match the weight of the wine to the weight of the food. For example, big, heavy winter dishes such as lasagne and roast meats, work well with big sturdy red wines. Light summer dishes, such as grilled white meat, seem to go best when accompanied by crisp and dry whites straight from the fridge.

The colour of the wine doesn't have to be the only factor. If we were to only drink white wines then we would need to match a heavier style white, one with oak ageing and probably a slightly higher alcohol

Thirsty work

level, to the heavier dish. If, conversely, we only partook in the old vin rouge then a lighter red, perhaps a chilled Gamay (the grape that makes Beaujolais) or even a nice Pinot Noir (an increasingly affordable option), would match better with more summery meals such as fresh free range chicken dishes.

The next factor to be considered is that of the sweetness level of the food. Again, in general terms, you need to match the dish with a wine at least as sweet. If the dish is sweeter then the wine will taste tart and thin. The best dessert wines are those that retain a refreshing acidity that balances the lush sweetness. Late harvest wines, especially Muscat's and Reislings, when served chilled are a real treat.

Alternatively a bottle of port offers a fantastic alternative for red wine enthusiasts. For those who love big succulent reds, a glass of port adds the sweetness needed to keep the taste buds on a par with the sweetness in the dessert.

The acid in the wine, usually more prevalent in white wines, needs to be matched to the acid in the food. If the acid in the food is higher then the wine will taste flabby and dull. Cooler climate wines (e.g. New Zealand and Northern Europe) and those made from grapes with a natural higher acidity (Sauvignon Blanc, Muscat and Riesling) are the most obvious choice for sharp and tangy dishes. As a red drinker, you would want cooler climate reds, low in tannin, light-bodied and with a nuance to be served chilled. The fatter the food becomes, with an introduction of heavier and richer sauces, especially cream, the less acidic and more rounded the wine should be.

Finally, the level of tannin, almost exclusively red wine orientated, needs to be taken into account when matching the wine to the dish. Tannin is the dry, mouth-coating texture present in both red wine and tea. It can overpower many foods that aren't heavy and chewy enough, but can be made unbearably dry when drunk with sweet dishes. Tannin levels are different within different red grape varieties. As a rule, the wines made from the heavier reds, Cabernet Sauvignon and Shiraz, have a higher tannin level so match better to robust food. Red wines lower in tannin, such as Gamay and Grenache, can hold up better against lighter dishes, and those with low tannin and high sugar (such as port or liqueur Muscats) match desserts and chocolate.

Wine, like food, does seem to have seasonal highs and lows. Chilled rosés and whites are great outside in the heady days of summer whilst that room temperature Rioja warms the cockles on a cold January evening. Whatever the time of year though it is worth using these basic principles to truly harmonise the union of the food, wine and cannabis.

Wine and menu suggestions

Summer

Shish kebab (see page 32)

This spicy dish requires a wine to balance and compliment.
Shiraz based wines, either single varietal or blended with Grenache or
Cabernet Sauvignon, would work nicely.

Ice cream (see page 39)

Weeds and wines with at least as much sweetness. I particularly
recommend the orange and flora muscats from Australia and California
or sparkling Asti (both should be nice and cold).

Savoury bread and butted pudding (see page 45)

As this is an egg-based dish a medium weight Chardonnay, such as
White Burgundy or South-East Australian, would be perfect.

Autumn

Any cheese pasties (see page 52)

A great match for port, especially late bottled vintage and tawny styles.

International feta parcels (see page 55)

Needs something sharp and clean, such as Sauvignon Blanc, especially
those from the Loire valley in France.

Green sea soup (see page 56)

Soup is always a difficult match, but if the Green sea has a hint of
saltiness then a Fino or Manzanilla sherry are suggested.

Cous cous with roasted vegetables (see page 64)

Requires wines with a naturally high zesty acidity, such as Gerwurtztraminer or dry/off-dry Rieslings or a chilled dry rose.

Winter

Turkey and herb stuffing (see page 74)

A Pinot Noir wine is a great match for this dish. The best in the world come from Burgundy, so look out for a bargain.

Vegetarian lasagne (see page 79)

Goes with any juicy Italian reds. A rising star is the Primitivo Grape which makes rich warming wines with a hint of sweetness.

A pot of hot pot (see page 82)

When cooking this dish use a wine that isn't too acidic or floral, something fairly basic that hasn't been open too long. To drink with the meal go for a nice spicy Shiraz or Rioja.

Spring

Pizza – stilton and broccoli (see page 135)

A nice juicy Grenache based wine such as Cotes du Rhone would work with this tomato and stilton based dish.

Jacket potatoes with cannabutter (see page 138)

The saltiness of this dish would ideally partner a red wine low in tannin, such as Beaujolais, or even an off-dry rosé.

After dinner or anytime

With chocolates fudge pudding, fudges, sweetmeats and truffles – Muscats or ports or a sparkling Asti are just what you want.

Tempt you to the table

Freshly cooked

Weights and measurements

Grams	Ounces	UK
0.75	1/32	1/2 tsp
1.75	1/16	1/2 tsp
3.5	1/8	1 tsp
7	1/4	
14	1/2	1tbs
25	1	
50	2	4tbs
85	3	
110	4 (1/4 lb)	
140	5	
175	6	
200	7	
225	8 (1/2 lb)	
450	16 (1 lb)	

UK pint	Fluid oz	Millilitre
1/2 tsp		2.5ml
1tsp		5ml
1tbs		15ml
1/4 pint	5	150ml
1/2 pint	10	300ml
1 pint	20	600ml
1 3/4 pint		1 litre

American measurements

Food type	Grams	Cups
Butter	225	1
Cheese	115	1
Currants	150	1
Dried fruits	150	1
Flour	115	1
Honey	350	1
Meat	225	1
Nuts	150	1
Dried pulses	225	1
Rice, raw	200	1
Cous cous	180	1
Sugar, white	225	1
Sugar, brown	200	1
Liquids	225ml	1

NB Many of the gram measurements used throughout the book have been rounded up or down, whichever is the most suitable and within the guidelines for food writers.

Oven temperatures

	Celsius	Fahrenheit	Gas
Very cool	110	225	¼
	120	250	½
Cool	140	275	1
	150	300	2
Moderate	160	325	3
	180	350	4
Moderately hot	190	375	5
	200	400	6
Very hot	220	425	7
	230	450	8

For fan assisted ovens reduce the temperatures by 10°c.

Safe measure

A spring cold

How cold you've gone since Spring!
Is this the time that you begin
To play your guessing games?
But not for me the tame.
Not those games for me,
If you care to be really free.

I've realised my lucky lot
Is put away on the shelf on top,
Sitting to ignore the pains,
Coagulating foggy brains.
Over, under, inside out,
Please speak your mind, but please
don't shout!

I'm far too young to fall and die.
You're far too old to sit and cry.
Raspberry and cold – shoulder pie,
The custard's for the other guy.

Peaceful days

By Alun Buffry
(Legalise Cannabis Alliance UK)

House rules

Max. 5g transaction a day per person

No hard drugs

No advertising

No nuisance

No minors

Help and advice always available